Know Your Christian Life

Sinclair B. Ferguson

A Theological Introduction

InterVarsity Press
Downers Grove
Illinois 60515

Copyright © 1981 by Sinclair B. Ferguson

Published in England under the title The Christian Life: A Doctrinal Introduction.
Printed in America by InterVarsity Press, Downers Grove, Illinois, with permission from Hodder and Stoughton Limited, Sevenoaks, Kent, England.

All rights reserved. No part of this book may be reproduced in any form without written permission from InterVarsity Press, Downers Grove, Illinois.

InterVarsity Press is the book-publishing division of Inter-Varsity Christian Fellowship, a student movement active on campus at hundreds of universities, colleges and schools of nursing. For information about local and regional activities, write IVCF, 233 Langdon St., Madison, WI 53703.

Cover photograph: Gary Irving

ISBN 0-87784-371-6

Printed in the United States of America

Library of Congress Cataloging in Publication Data

Ferguson, Sinclair B.
  Know your Christian life.

  Previously published as: The Christian life, 1981.
  1. Theology, Doctrinal–Popular works.
2. Christian life–Presbyterian authors.   I. Title.
BT77.F38   1981   230'.52   81-18588
ISBN 0-87784-371-6   AACR2

17	16	15	14	13	12	11	10	9	8	7	6	5	4	3	2	1
95	94	93	92	91	90	89	88	87	86	85	84	83	82	81		

To Dorothy
my best friend

1 Knowing Is for Living *1*
2 God's Broken Image *9*
3 The Plan of Grace *16*
4 Called by God *24*
5 Conviction of Sin *34*
6 Born Again *42*
7 Faith in Christ *55*
8 True Repentance *62*
9 Justification *71*
10 Sons of God *82*
11 Union with Christ *92*
12 Election *102*
13 Sin's Dominion Ended *116*
14 The Christian's Conflicts *126*
15 Crucifying Sin *138*
16 Perseverance *149*
17 Asleep in Christ *161*
18 Glorification *170*

Foreword

I am delighted to be composing the introductory fanfare for this book. It seems to me a fine piece of work, and one which does a job that needs doing. A wise man has said that your Christian life is like a three-legged stool. The legs are doctrine, experience and practice (that is, obedience), and you will not stay upright unless all three are there. In recent years, however, many Christian people have not kept these three together. Some have concentrated on doctrine (usually Calvinistic), some on experience (usually charismatic), some on practice (usually causes, good or less good), and the all-round Christlikeness which doctrine, experience and practice together would produce has not appeared. To say it the other way round, the imbalance of our efforts to honour the Holy Spirit as teacher or lord or leader seems actually to have quenched his influence, so that amid much talk and bustle we find little life and power. So to bring us back to biblical basics about the source, nature and expression of the Christian life is seasonable therapy; and that is the service which Dr Ferguson renders in the pages that follow.

Here is *theology*; but don't be frightened. Dr Ferguson is an accomplished divine in the best Scottish tradition, indeed the best tradition anywhere: so far from blinding us with the technicalities of theological science, he conceals the learning which his judgments reflect and sets everything before us in the form of straight exposition of Scripture, just as John Calvin and John Owen (not to name more) did before him. What he presents to us is thus *biblical* theology, and in its conclusions *reformed* theology, of the older, riper, wiser, deeper sort. Anyone who has read books II and III of Calvin's *Institutes* and the treatises on the Holy Spirit and the Christian life by John Owen will think he knows where Dr Ferguson got his ideas from; though the ideas themselves are drawn from Scripture with a skill that makes them as fresh and compelling as if one had never met them before. Moreover, the theology is *practical*, applying Bible teaching with insight and wisdom to the condition of plain people. It has been pointed out that Jesus told Peter to feed his lambs, not his giraffes, and this Dr Ferguson does, bringing everything down to simple essentials. Christian beginners will get the benefit and the Lord's older sheep, grown tough and stringy maybe, will find themselves edified and perhaps tenderised too.

Let no one complain that the teaching is old-fashioned. True or false, that is a triviality. What matters is whether it is true to the Bible and the realities of living. I think it is; so I commend the book with enthusiasm and gratitude, and shall look for more from Dr Ferguson's pen.

J. I. Packer
REGENT COLLEGE
VANCOUVER,
CANADA

Introduction

The demand for books on Christian doctrine is like the tide of the sea; it ebbs and flows. For a period of time there may be a great deal of doctrinal teaching received by Christians in books, sermons and by other means, only to produce a reaction from doctrine to experience. Then the tide which flows in on the next day of the church's life brings with it a variety of books on Christian experience. Rarely do we manage to catch the balance.

But in the last decade observers have begun to notice a new desire among Christians for a solid foundation upon which experience may be built. The kind of Christian preaching and literature which has been in demand has imperceptibly begun to change, and there is a new hunger for doctrinal teaching which is married to experience.

It is my prayerful hope that these pages will make some small contribution to this exciting situation. I have chosen their theme quite consciously because the Christian life is common ground for all Christians, however familiar or otherwise general Christian doctrine is to them. These chapters by their very nature already have one foot in a shared Christian experience, and in many ways provide the obvious starting point for any Christian who wants to study Christian doctrine. *The Christian Life* is not a text book, or manual of doctrine as such, but in many chapters extensive use of Scripture is made, and in some cases more detailed study of certain vital passages. Quotations, unless indicated otherwise, are from the *New International Version*. It will certainly increase the value of reading if a copy of Scripture is near at hand for consultation.

I am grateful to those who have encouraged me during the writing of these studies. In particular I am indebted to the Rev. Robert Horn for his helpful comments on the original manuscript; to Miss Alison Hair for helping so willingly in typing the material; to Dr. James I. Packer for writing the Foreword and most of all to my wife Dorothy, and our three boys, David,

Peter and John. They have all contributed in their own ways to enable me to produce these pages, and together have provided the companionship with which God daily sustains me.

SINCLAIR B. FERGUSON
GLASGOW, AUGUST 1980

1
Knowing Is for Living

When I first became involved in teaching God's word, I tended to assume that one of the great needs of Christians is to be instructed in the 'deeper truths' of the gospel. It was not long before experience (of my own life) and observation (of others' lives) taught me how mistaken I had been. I began to see that in fact the 'deeper truths' (if there are such things) are really the old basic truths of the gospel. Far from being luxuries, they are necessities for Christian living. The rather disturbing thought began to dawn on me that many of us who are professing Christians are distressingly weak in our grasp of the basic framework of biblical doctrine. We assume that we know the elements of the message of the New Testament, but sometimes our understanding of them is like that of a child.

As I began to ponder on this situation I realised that, perhaps, it was not very different from the conditions with which the apostle Paul was faced. I remembered his repeated question in the Letter to the Romans and the First Letter to the Corinthians: 'Do you not know? ... do you not know?' (Rom. 6:3, 16; 7:1; 1 Cor. 3:16; 5:6; 6:2, 3, 9, 15, 19; 9:13, 24). *Over and over again he had appealed to what these early Christians ought to have known, but had either forgotten or never learned.*

The conviction that Christian doctrine matters for Christian living is one of the most important *growth points* of the Christian life.

Frequently in pastoral work this can be seen. Most of us, by nature, are not students but more 'practical' types, 'doers' rather than 'thinkers'. Yet both Scripture and the history of the church indicate to us that it is generally speaking 'thinkers' who make the best 'doers'! Cast your mind over the life-stories of the men and women who have had the most practical influences on the church, or perhaps on your own life. You will discover very few among them who were not students of Christian truth, however unsophisticatedly they went about their studies. From the greatest theologians, martyrs and intellectually gifted preachers, to those of lowliest gifts but spiritual power, all, perhaps without exception, have been students of the doctrines of the Bible, and therein lies one of the secrets of their usefulness. However paradoxical it seems to our natural minds, it is one of the facts of spiritual reality that practical Christian living is based on understanding and knowledge. A verse in the Old Testament illustrates this. It says of man that 'as he thinks within himself, so he is' (Prov. 23:7 N.I.V. margin). That summarises the Christian position perfectly—how we think is one of the great determining factors in how we live!

It is not difficult to demonstrate that this conviction underlies the whole of the teaching of the New Testament.

The Teaching of Jesus

Jesus taught practical Christianity in the Sermon on the Mount. To some people it has not seemed very *practicable*, but it certainly speaks from start to finish about day-to-day realities! Here we find instruction on how to behave, on the motivations which lie behind our actions, on prayer, anxiety and many other practical matters. But on what foundation are these practical realities to be built? Jesus teaches that they rest on what we know of God, his nature and the ways in which he deals with men. The great motive for prayer our Lord lays before us is that we know that God is the Father (and we are therefore his children) and that he knows what we need before we ask. The pattern prayer Christ gave us is a manual of doctrine if ever there was one—the Fatherhood of God, his heavenly existence, his holiness, his name, his kingdom and its coming, the nature of the divine will, his daily providence, his forgiveness, the problem of temptation and the existence of the Devil! The Sermon on the Mount, Christ's 'Design for Life in the Kingdom of God' as it has been called, is an unashamedly doctrinal sermon. The message is that the knowledge of God and the sure understanding of his character and ways provide the basis for all practical Christian living.

The same is true of Jesus' other great sermons. In Matthew 24–25, Mark 13 and Luke 22:5–36, we have a record of what is sometimes called 'The Little Apocalypse'. It is our Lord's teaching on 'the last things'. But the striking thing about his doctrine is how practical its repercussions are. Christ did not impart knowledge for its own sake to his small band of followers. He taught them to enable them to live in a truly Christian way whatever the circumstances of their lives.

This is all the clearer in Jesus' last sermon to the eleven gathered in the upper room (recorded in John 13–17). Here he is facing his own greatest crisis. He is 'troubled in spirit' (Jn. 13:21). His disciples were also obviously under great pressure and in distress. Their hearts were also troubled (Jn. 14:1, 27). What does Jesus do? How does he respond? Our Lord himself concentrates on what we would nowadays regard as the highest and grandest of Christian doctrines!

Jesus' mind soars to the doctrine of the Trinity: 'I will ask the Father, and he will give you another Counsellor to be with you for ever—the Spirit of truth' (Jn. 14:16–17); 'If you really knew me, you would know my Father as well ... Anyone who has seen me has seen the Father ... I am in the Father and the Father is in me' (Jn. 14:7, 9, 10). 'All that belongs to the Father is mine. That is why I said the Spirit will take from what is mine and make it known to you' (Jn. 16:15). *Our Lord also concentrates on the thought of the glory of God*: 'Now is the Son of Man glorified and God is glorified in him. If God is glorified in him, then God will glorify the Son in himself, and glorify him at once' (Jn. 13:31-2). 'Father, the time has come. Glorify your Son, that your Son may glorify you' (Jn. 17:1). 'Father, I want those you have given me to be with me where I am, and to see my glory, the glory you have given me because you loved me before the creation of the world' (Jn. 17:24).

How do we begin to explore the riches of such statements?

The point to be underscored is that these great truths, which we tend to isolate in a category of 'doctrines', are in fact the very foundation of Jesus' encouragement of his disciples and even himself in an hour of great practical need. It is as though he were saying: 'Only the man who has a grasp of these heights will be able to hold firm when he descends to the depths of human experience.' We must therefore, in the light of this, recognise how practically important Christian doctrines are.

We may have to rethink our personal response to doctrine in

order to integrate it into the very warp and woof of our spiritual experience. For too many Christians for too long, 'doctrine' has been thought of as impractical, stodgy and relatively useless. But we cannot obediently hear our Lord (surely the most practical Man who ever lived), if we turn away from his doctrine. For he teaches doctrine in order to fill our lives with stability and grace.

THE TEACHING OF PAUL

Can the man who wrote these words be regarded as impractical?

> I have worked much harder, been in prison more frequently, been flogged more severely, and been exposed to death again and again. Five times I received from the Jews the forty lashes minus one. Three times I was beaten with rods, once I was stoned, three times I was shipwrecked, I spent a night and a day in the open sea, I have been constantly on the move. I have been in danger from rivers, in danger from bandits, in danger from my own countrymen, in danger from Gentiles; in danger in the city, in danger in the country, in danger at sea; and in danger from false brothers. I have laboured and toiled and have often gone without sleep; I have known hunger and thirst and have often gone without food; I have been cold and naked. Besides everything else, I face daily the pressure of my concern for all the churches.
>
> 2 Corinthians 11:23-28

What sustained Paul under these pressures? There is only one possible answer. He had a vital knowledge of the character of God, the work of Christ, the nature of God's ways, and the indwelling power of the Holy Spirit. His life was characterised by the power which the truth released in his experience. This is why his appeals to the early churches are so poignant: 'Do you not know?' he asks; 'If only you knew and understood, then your lives would be so different!' No text from his writings brings this out more clearly than J. B. Phillips' famous rendering of Romans 12:1-2:

With eyes wide open to the mercies of God, I beg you, my brothers, as an act of intelligent worship, to give him your bodies, as a living sacrifice, consecrated to him and acceptable by him. Don't let the world around you squeeze you into its own mould, but let God re-mould your minds from within, so that you may prove in practice that the plan of God for you is good, meets all his demands and moves towards the goal of true maturity.

Here are all the essential elements of a life of devoted loyalty to Christ. But perhaps the most astonishing thing is the plea these words contain: Christians, use your minds! Give your bodies to the Lord 'as an act of *intelligent* worship'. Let 'God re-mould your *minds* from within'.

We will respond with the kind of sharp-edged consecration which proves fruitful in Christian living only as our eyes are wide open to the mercies of God. As we understand and appreciate the mercies of God we will live more fully for Christ. *But what are the mercies of God?* How can we understand them? The answer is that God's mercies have been expounded in Romans 1–11, by common consent the most doctrinal section in all Paul's writings! As we grapple with the teaching in these pages our eyes will be opened wide to the expansiveness of God's grace in our salvation. As we begin to taste the sheer wonder of what has been done for us, and sink ourselves more deeply into the resources of grace which are explained there to us, consecration and practical Christian living will become more meaningful to us.

Earlier in Romans Paul firmly underlined that this is not an optional extra for Christians. It is a basic necessity. In Romans 6:17, he speaks of Christians being delivered up to a 'form of doctrine'. The word which is translated 'form' means *a mould*. As a child I spent many hours making plaster of paris models with the help of rubber moulds—rather unsuccessfully! We poured the soft plaster into the mould and waited for it to set. My favourite was a clown who usually appeared without a nose! What joy there was when a perfect reproduction appeared from the mould. This is the picture Paul has in mind. 'Now', he is saying, 'when you became a Christian your life was melted down by God to be entirely reshaped by his grace, and moulded by this "form of doctrine".' The doctrines of the gospel are meant to mould us so that our lives begin to 'set' in the likeness of Christ.

In a sense we might say that the letter to the Romans gives us the broad outline of this mould. It shows us the shape of God's grace to us in Christ, and when we begin to understand its teaching, it makes powerful impressions upon our lives and daily conduct. It determines the way we live. But surely many Christians have lived their lives without much grasp of Christian truth and it has made very little difference? Often that is the unfortunate truth! Our lives have been no different from our contemporaries'. We have made little or no impression upon the world, for the very reason that gospel doctrine has made a correspondingly slight impression upon us. It cannot be overemphasised that men and women who have accomplished anything in God's strength have always done so on the basis of their grasp of truth. They themselves may not have described their approach as 'doctrinal', thinking often of themselves simply as students of God's word. Yet, it has been because of their appreciation of biblical doctrine that they have been useful instruments in the hands of God.

In effect this is the lesson Paul underlined for his young friend Timothy when he described the character and value of Scripture to him:

> But as for you, continue in what you have learned and have become convinced of, because you know those from whom you learned it, and how from infancy you have known the holy Scriptures, which are able to make you wise unto salvation through faith in Christ Jesus. All Scripture is God-breathed and is useful for teaching, rebuking, correcting and training in righteousness, so that the man of God may be thoroughly equipped for every good work.
>
> 2 Timothy 3:14–17

Notice Paul's connection between Scripture, teaching and training, and the practicalities of being a Christian soldier 'kitted out' 'for every good work'. At the end of the day all doctrine has this essentially practical quality about it. It forms our thinking in such a way that it becomes a determining factor in our living.

Our Doctrine Should Be Practical

The studies which follow are unashamedly doctrinal. This is not to suggest that we should play down the importance of experience. The very reverse is true. As we find our minds expanded by the grace of God, our hearts should be correspondingly enlarged with love for him for all that he has done for us in Christ. This in turn should lead us to a richer experience of his love for us. We ought not to fall into the trap of thinking that we put doctrine in its right place simply by ignoring experience. Nor should we despise spiritual experiences. On the contrary, we should rejoice in them. But we only ultimately benefit from experiences when we trace the great doctrinal principles which they illustrate.

The chapters which follow concentrate attention on the doctrines which surround the Christian life. They do not provide a manual of systematic theology which covers every conceivable biblical doctrine. Rather they attempt to provide a biblical exposition of the doctrines which interpret our Christian experience and with which we have some kind of familiarity. These truths will begin to open up for us the greatness of salvation. They will prevent us from being dogged with that common inferiority-complex Christian mentality which thinks that the experience of being a Christian is a very mundane and ordinary thing. But most of all, these doctrines are character-building and life-changing. Most of them are key doctrines in the growth and development of the Christian life.

It is one of the enigmas of our day that in a world of great opportunities, many Christians have less knowledge of Christian doctrine than children at Sunday school had in previous centuries. That is probably a fact, even if it may be retorted that the children of past generations could not conceivably have grasped the doctrine they were taught in their catechisms (itself a debatable point!). It may also be one reason for the differences between the quality of Christian character of previous eras and the relatively poor standard of our own Christian lives today.

No illustration pin-points the intangible quality of the power of Christian doctrine to mould character and life better than the exquisite story related by the famous American theologian Benjamin B. Warfield. It speaks for itself:

> We have the following bit of personal experience from a general officer of the United States army. He was in a great western city at a time of intense excitement and violent rioting. The streets were over-run daily by a dangerous crowd. One day he observed approaching him a man of singularly combined calmness and firmness of mien, whose very demeanor inspired confidence. So impressed was he with his bearing amid the surrounding uproar that when he had passed he turned to look back at him, only to find that the stranger had done the same. On observing his turning the stranger at once came back to him, and touching his chest with his forefinger, demanded without preface: 'What is the chief end of man?' [the first question in the Shorter Catechism]. On receiving the countersign, 'Man's chief end is to glorify God and to enjoy him for ever' [the Catechism's answer] — 'Ah!' said he, 'I knew you were a Shorter Catechism boy by your looks!' 'Why, that was just what I was thinking of you,' was the rejoinder.
>
> *Selected Shorter Writings*, I, p. 383–4

It is in this way that our understanding of Christian doctrine shapes Christian life. It even begins to influence our unconscious bearing and our responses to all kinds of situations. Christian doctrines are life-shaping. They show us the God we worship, and illuminate our understanding of his Son's love and his Spirit's work. They form the foundation of the Christian life.

2
God's Broken Image

Bishop J. C. Ryle's most famous book, *Holiness* begins with these well chosen words:

> He that wishes to attain right views about Christian holiness, must begin by examining the vast and solemn subject of *sin*. He must dig down very low if he would build high. A mistake here is most mischievous. Wrong views about holiness are generally traceable to wrong views about human corruption. I make no apology for beginning this volume of papers about holiness by making some plain statements about sin.
>
> The plain truth is that a right knowledge of sin lies at the root of all saving Christianity. Without it such doctrines as justification, conversion, sanctification, are 'words and names' which convey no meaning to the mind. The first thing therefore, that God does when he makes anyone a new creature in Christ, is to send light into his heart, and show him that he is a guilty sinner.
>
> *Holiness*, p. 1

How right Ryle was! He was right not only doctrinally, but particularly at the level of practical Christian experience. Only as we begin to appreciate what we were before we became Christians (or what we would be naturally were we not Christians), do we begin to sense something of the immense grandeur of being new creatures in Christ. We would still need the love and tenderness of God even if man had not fallen into guilt and corruption. But the great burden of the gospel is that our situation is infinitely more serious and critical. *We will never properly understand the work of God which takes place in the Christian life unless we first of all have some kind of grasp of why we need the grace of God.*

THE EFFECTS OF SIN

Scripture employs a rich variety of expression to convey a sense of the disintegration of our relationships with God, our fellows, the world around us and ourselves. Sin is missing the mark or the goal which God has appointed, and falling short of the glory of God which we were created to enjoy (see Rom. 3:23). It means to deviate from the right path and to find ourselves under a verdict of guilty in the presence of the Eternal Judge. It means, plainly, to be a rebel against a rightful and loving King. It is to be a traitor to the goodness of God (Rom. 3:10–18).

But there are four fundamental emphases which illuminate the sad condition in which men now find themselves.

(i) The image of God defaced

Genesis 1:26–7 introduces us to the original divine pattern for man's life. He was the image-bearer of God:

> Then God said, 'Let us make man in our image, in our likeness, and let them rule over the fish of the sea and the birds of the air, over the livestock, over all the earth, and over all the creatures that move along the ground.'
> So God created man in his own image, in the image of God he created him; male and female he created them.

In the history of the church there have been many views about the meaning of 'the image of God'. Does God have physical and bodily characteristics? Or should we look for a trinity of human qualities which might display the three-in-oneness of God? Is it perhaps that man has a capacity for reasoning and verbal communication, so like the God who speaks his word to men? The 'image of God' probably means that God originally made man to reflect his holy character and his position as bearing rightful rule over all his creation. In that respect he is like God.

It is an amazing thing to think of man set in the world in order to be God's personal representative upon the earth. The opening chapters of Genesis breathe something of this quiet spirit of wonder. Man is given creative powers (Gen. 1:28); he exercises dominion (Gen. 1:26); like God he is a creative workman (Gen. 2:15).

But in Genesis 3 something happens in each of these areas to distort God's gracious plan. A virulent disease begins to spread through the whole of man's life from the first moment of his sin. He hides from God in the garden (Gen. 3:8–10); his relationship with his wife, and hers with him, is distorted into one of ugly, back-biting recrimination (Gen. 3:13–17); the ground is cursed and man's daily labour becomes a burden rather than a pleasure (Gen. 3:17-19). All this is sad enough, but it is accompanied by a change in the image of God.

Theologians have often discussed an interesting question here. Does Scripture teach that man is no longer in the image of God? Or does it suggest that the image remains but has been grossly defaced? In many ways that is an even more tragic prospect. We might well be justified in thinking that there could be no greater disaster than that the likeness of God should be exterminated. But in fact there is. What if the image of God, in which his greatness and glory is reflected, becomes a distortion of his character? What if, instead of reflecting his glory, man begins to reflect the very antithesis of God? What if God's image becomes an anti-god? This, essentially, is the affront which fallen man is to God. He takes all that God has lavished upon him to enable him to live in free and joyful obedience, and he transforms it into a weapon by which he can oppose his Maker. The very breath which God gives him thousands of times each day he abuses by his sin. The magnitude of his sin is also the measure of his need of salvation. The wonder of God's saving purpose lies in the fact that he longs more than we imagine to restore what has been lost. But the old creation must pass away, and a new be established; what was lost in Adam must be restored in Christ if there is to be any hope of sharing the glory of God from which we have fallen. Perhaps no writer has caught this perspective more clearly than John Calvin:

> Adam was at first created in the image of God, so that he might reflect, as in a mirror, the righteousness of God. But that image, having been wiped out by sin, must now be restored in Christ. The regeneration of the godly is indeed, as is said in 2 Cor. 3:18, nothing else than the reformation of the image of God in them. But there is a far more rich and powerful grace of God in this second creation than in the first ... Adam lost the image which he had originally received, therefore it is necessary that it shall be restored to us by Christ. Therefore he teaches that the design in regeneration is to lead us back from error to that end for which we were created.
> *Commentary on Galatians, Ephesians, Philippians and Colossians*, p. 191

(ii) Man under the dominion of sin and death

The threat of sin and death appeared early in the narrative of Genesis. By the command of Genesis 2:17 man was, as it were, put on a probationary period by God: 'You must not eat from the tree of the knowledge of good and evil, for when you eat of it you will surely die.' But Satan came in serpent-guise to destroy the divine-human fellowship. He attacked the suggestion that man would come under the dominion of death—'You will not surely die' (Gen. 3:4). He also undermined the goodness of God by his suggestion that God grudged their presence in his garden (Gen. 3:4–5). The rest of Genesis 3 narrates the sad tale of man's yielding to temptation, and by the time we turn another page we discover that 'sin is crouching at your door; it desires to have you' (Gen. 4:7). The picture is of sin as a wild animal, waiting to pounce upon its hapless victim. The same truth appears in different words in the teaching of Jesus: 'Everyone who sins is a slave to sin' (Jn. 8:34). Paul emphasises the same point in Romans: men are 'under sin', as slaves. Indeed in Romans 5:12–6:23 the references to sin in the Greek are usually to *The Sin*, as though it had taken on personal proportions.

As a consequence men are powerless. Even when the will is strong, yet 'the evil I do not want to do—this I keep on doing' (Rom. 7:19). The result is eloquently expressed in the same epistle:

> The mind of sinful man is death ... because the sinful mind is hostile to God. It does not submit to God's law, *nor can it do so.*
>
> Rom. 8:6–8

(iii) Man guilty before God

These first two dimensions of man's condition draw our attention to the effects of sin in his own life. But the Scriptures also emphasise that his relationship to God is distorted by his sin. Man is guilty. Not only does he suffer the consequences of sin in human misery, but he comes under the condemnation of God.

We find the clearest exposition of this in Romans. In Romans 2:1–16, Paul outlines the principles which God employs in coming to a verdict on our lives. He shows that God's judgment is always according to truth and reality (v. 2); that it is given in accordance with works (v. 6), and also is tempered by the light of revelation which men have received (vv. 12–15). It is a judgment which will be administered through Christ (v. 16) and therefore will take account of all the secrets of men's hearts. Sometimes these words have been taken to indicate the lenient attitude of God in his judgment. But that is to misunderstand God, and to fail to understand Paul. At this point in the letter he is demonstrating the guilt of all men before God. These principles are the instruments by which the true nature of our sin will be made plain. We have no works to justify us. We have failed to live according to the light God has given us. By the standard of Christ's life we are guilty sinners. Thus God's judgment is according to the truth! On any one of these principles of judgment Paul can argue for a verdict of guilty and a sentence of condemnation. No excuses will be valid on that Day when men appear at the Last Assize. Every mouth will be closed and all men will be declared guilty before God (Rom. 3:19).

Paul does not mean that men *feel* a great sense of guilt. Whether they do or not is beside the point. He is describing the divine verdict, not the human psychology. But something yet more terrible accompanies this verdict, for on its shoulders comes the wrath of God revealed from heaven against godlessness and wickedness (Rom. 1:18). Apart from Christ, says the apostle of love, 'God's wrath remains' (Jn. 3:36).

(iv) Man in the grip of Satan

It is an axiom in the Bible that the greater the light of God's revelation, the sharper the darkness of opposition to it. The light shows the true nature of the darkness. In terms of the exposing of the powers of evil this is undoubtedly true. In the Old Testament we find references to Satan and his work, and hints about his character and evil purposes. But it is only in the full light of Christ that he seems to be drawn out into the open, unmasked and identified. Consequently in the New Testament we find such illuminating passages as Ephesians 2:1–4, in which men are seen not only as living a lifeless death in sin, dominated by the course and fashions of this world, but are described as being under the dominion of the devil. John goes so far as to suggest that the whole world lies in his power, underlining Jesus' description of Satan as 'the prince of this world' (1 Jn. 5:19 cf. Jn. 12:31; 16:11). The ultimate tragedy of man's self-understanding is that he believes himself to be free, has all the feelings of a free agent, but does not realise that he is a slave to sin and serves the will of Satan.

What then are the basic needs which are met in the message of the gospel?

(i) *We need re-creation* by Christ in order that the image of God, once distorted by sin, may be restored. (ii) *We need deliverance* from the dominion of sin in order that we may live freely for God. (iii) *We need to be rescued from the power of Satan* so that our lives may be given to Christ the Lord as his glad bondslaves. (iv) *We need to be saved from the wrath of God* so that, released from this most terrifying of all prospects, we may live the life of forgiven sinners.

SALVATION

It is the glory of the gospel that it meets our need. It comes to us in our sin and begins to undo what had been wrongly done in our lives in order that God's image may be restored. But it also pronounces us already to be, in Christ, what we will be in ourselves only when we are transformed by the last great crisis into his perfect image (1 Jn. 3:1–3). Perhaps the most wonderful thing of all is that God lifts us not only from what we are by nature to what Adam was in the Garden of Eden, but to what Adam was to become in the presence of God, and would have been had he persevered in obedience. The gospel does not make us like Adam in his innocence—it makes us like Christ, in all the perfection of his reflection of God. This is the essence of the salvation Christ provides, and it undergirds the pattern of Christian experience and doctrine which we find in the New Testament (Rom. 8:29).

But how is such a salvation provided by Christ? He came into the world as the Second Man, the Last Adam (1 Cor. 15:45, 47). Out of his perfect reflection of the image of God we may draw by the power of the Holy Spirit. We share in his death to the dominion of sin (Rom. 6:10). Under him we shelter from the wrath of God, knowing that he has borne our guilt (Gal. 3:13).

He was made sin for us although he himself knew no sin, so that in him we might be made the righteousness of God (2 Cor. 5:21). He died, the just for the unjust, to bring us to God (1 Pet. 3:18). On the Cross he triumphed over Satan, and exposed him as our enemy (Col. 2:15). In his name therefore we may also conquer (Rev. 12:10). Christ is our wisdom, righteousness, sanctification and redemption (1 Cor. 1:30). All we shall ever need we will find he supplies by his grace.

There are then only two questions which remain to be answered. The answers to them form the substance of all that follows in these pages:

How do I get into Christ, to receive this salvation which is in him? We will find the answer to this by examining the biblical teaching on entering into the Christian life.

How do I get the grace and character of Christ into my life? We will explore the answer to this as we go on to consider the biblical teaching on sanctification and the outworking of the Christian life.

3
The Plan of Grace

Students of Christian doctrine used to speak about what they called the *order*, or *plan of salvation*. They meant that in his dealings with men God worked according to a pattern which was more or less invariable. In simple terms, he had a plan. They did not mean, of course, that God's ways are stereotyped, or that he deals with men simply as numbers on a computer programme. They meant that sinners restored to the image of God will have their experience of God's grace in basically similar ways because ultimately their needs are the same.

It may help us to see that such a plan can be a deeply personal thing if we recall that God employed a careful strategy in the life of his own Son. The incarnation did not take place by accident or afterthought. The life of Jesus was not one of chance. Over and over again Jesus clearly referred to a pattern and goal by which his life was determined. He liked to think of it as heading towards a special hour in which everything for which he was preparing himself would be accomplished. He held back from certain activities because of his consciousness of the divine time-table (Jn. 2:4; 7:30; 8:20; 12:23, 27). But by the beginning of the 'book of the passion' (Jn. 13–21) Jesus knew that 'the time had come to leave the world and go to the Father' (Jn. 13:1), and so he prayed, 'Father, the time has come' (Jn. 17:1).

This perspective on our Lord's life was a dominant theme in the understanding of the early church as they looked back upon his passion. Not even his death was an accident. *Indeed, of all events, his death was no accident.* In the first sermon on the Day of Pentecost Peter indicated this—'This man was handed over to you *by God's set purpose and foreknowledge*' (Acts 2:23). Later when the persecuted church lifted its heart to God in prayer the same emphasis was repeated:

> Indeed Herod and Pontius Pilate met together with the Gentiles and the people of Israel in this city to conspire

against your holy servant Jesus, whom you anointed. They did *what your power and will had decided beforehand* should happen.

Acts 4:27-8

The Plan of God

It is fundamental to all Christian thinking to believe that God is a planning God. Our Lord himself lived in the comfort of this knowledge. We ought not to find it a frustration to take this yoke upon our own lives.

The Bible indicates clearly in different ways that God's plan for the lives of his children has certain fixed points. To understand the full depth of what God has done for us in Christ we must explore this saving plan. Before we go on to consider the meaning of the great biblical words we associate with the Christian life, such as Justification, Regeneration, Sanctification and so on, we must try to trace out how these doctrines and the experience which they describe are related to each other.

This procedure has its dangers, the most obvious being that once we have established an *understanding* of God's grace and its pattern in our lives we may mistake that for the *experience* of God's grace. But there is a world of difference between *knowledge of the truth* in this systematic sense and a personal *experience of its powers*. There is also the danger that we will want to fit everything into a pattern when Scripture may not provide us with sufficient information to do so. But, on the other hand there are many benefits to be gained by such an exercise. One major blessing is that it offers us a divine perspective on our lives. It lifts our eyes up from our own small measures of the experience of God's grace to show us the largeness of the purposes he cherishes. We then discover, as Paul says, that 'our salvation is nearer now than when we first believed' (Rom. 13:11), and also that it is greater now than when we first believed!

There are three passages in particular where the New Testament reflects on the whole of salvation viewed from the perspective of its different parts.

(i) *Romans 8:28-30*

And we know that in all things God works for the good of

those who love him, wwho have been called according to his purpose. For those God foreknew he also predestined to be conformed to the likeness of his Son, that he might be the firstborn among many brothers. And those he predestined, he also called; those he called, he also justified; those he justified, he also glorified.

We will return to these verses at a later stage of our study, but at this juncture the main lines of their significance may be drawn. It is clear, in the first place, that the plan of salvation, what Paul here calls 'purpose', is a source of great encouragement to the child of God. These heavily-weighted theological words, 'purpose', 'foreknowledge', 'predestination', 'calling', 'justification', 'glorification' were not dictated by a man who was interested in theology in the same way we might have an interest in doing cross-word puzzles. One cannot set cross-word puzzles to music, but these words lend themselves to song. There is a marching beat to them. There is something seriously wrong with our understanding of Scripture if we regard them primarily as a source of theological controversy.

Consider what they say. In general terms they teach us that nothing ever escapes from the over-arching purpose of God for his people. Indeed, not only do all the circumstances of my life not take God by surprise, but he actually employs them for my blessing. He works them together like a Master Knitter gathering together the many-coloured strands of wool. He puts into effect an intricate design which will be made clear only when the finished garment is held up to the admiring onlookers. This itself is a comfort in the darkest hour.

Paul is intent on explaining the rationale which lies in the divine mind. How can all things be worked together by God for good? The answer is at hand. It is because God's *ultimate purpose* is to make us like Christ. His goal is the complete restoration of the image of God in his child! So great a work demands all the resources which God finds throughout the universe, and he ransacks the possibilities of joys and sorrows in order to reproduce in us the character of Jesus. But the question arises: With such poor material, how can God guarantee the glorious finished articles? The answer is that for all the differences which mark the followers of Christ, some things are always true of them. They have been foreknown by God, and he has predestined them. He has called them into his kingdom and justified them. It is these who will bear the image of his Son on the Day of Glory.

Paul's statement provides us with certain fixed points of reference. His words are applicable to all Christians ('those who love him'). What is common to them is that on the basis of his foreknowledge God has predestined, called, justified and glorified them. The apostle is stretching out before us the dimensions of God's saving grace. Its full expanse is seen in the divine plan of salvation. His love for us began before the dawning of time and extends until time's last rolling year has gone:

> *Who then can e'er divide us more*
> *from Jesus and his love,*
> *Or break the sacred chain that binds*
> *the earth to heav'n above?*
>
> *Let troubles rise, and terrors frown*
> *and days of darkness fall;*
> *Through him all dangers we'll defy*
> *and more than conquer all.*
>
> *Nor death nor life, nor earth nor hell,*
> *nor time's destroying sway,*
> *Can e'er efface us from his heart*
> *or make his love decay.*

It is important for us to see that such eloquent confidence is only possible on the basis of an appreciation of the basic elements in the plan of grace.

(ii) *Ephesians 1:3–14*

Praise be to the God and Father of our Lord Jesus Christ, who has blessed us in the heavenly realms with every spiritual blessing in Christ. For he chose us in him before the creation of the world to be holy and blameless in his sight. In love he predestined us to be adopted as his sons through Jesus Christ, in accordance with his pleasure and will—to the praise of his glorious grace, which he has freely given us in the One he loves. In him we have redemption through his blood, the forgiveness of sins, in accordance with the riches of God's grace that he lavished on us with all wisdom and understanding. And he made known to us the mystery of his will according to his good pleasure, which he purposed in Christ, to be put into effect when the times have reached their fulfilment—to bring all things in heaven and on earth together under one head, even Christ.

In him we were also chosen, having been predestined according to the plan of him who works out everything in conformity with the purpose of his will, in order that we, who were the first to hope in Christ, might be for the praise of his glory. And you also were included in Christ when you heard the word of truth, the gospel of your salvation. Having believed, you were marked in him with a seal, the promised Holy Spirit, who is a deposit guaranteeing our inheritance until the redemption of those who are God's possession—to the praise of his glory.

If Romans 8 could be sung, these verses definitely should be sung! They even carry a chorus, 'to the praise of his glory'. Like Romans 8:28–30 they have often been scrutinised because they reflect on the eternal counsels of God. But let us revel in the sunshine as believers before we try to analyse it as scientific theologians! The legitimate investigation of the latter should not dull the pleasures of the former.

In Ephesians Paul is approaching the subject of salvation quite differently from the method he adopted in Romans. There the whole letter opens out from the starting place of man's deep-seated need under the wrath and condemnation of God. It is only when he has expounded that need, the divine answer to it in grace, and the resources which are ours in Christ, that Paul traces all this back to the eternal purpose of God as he *closes* the first major section of the letter with his paean of praise in Romans 8. Ephesians, by contrast, *begins* with that plan of salvation, and rather than describing its chronological outworking (foreknowledge and predestination *leading to* calling, justification, glorification as in Romans 8), Paul states its Christological centre: all spiritual blessings are ours *in Christ*. In Romans 8 the great doctrines are links in a chain. In Ephesians 1 they are spokes in a wheel which centres on Christ. In Christ we are *blessed, chosen, predestined to be sons, engraced, enlightened, included, sealed.* The emphasis here is not entirely chronological. Rather Paul is drawing out the fulness of the grace which becomes ours when we become Christ's. None the less it will be noticed that Paul does add other dimensions to those we noticed in Romans 8:28–30. In Ephesians 1:13–14, he indicates that believing follows upon calling, and also seems to indicate that receiving the Holy Spirit is the experience of those who have come to believe in Jesus. He has therefore begun to expand our original map of God's purposes. If we were now to enlarge Romans 8:30, it might read: 'Those God chose and predestined he also called; those he called through his word came to believe, were justified and were sealed with the Spirit. These same are also glorified.'

(iii) *John 1:12–13*
Yet to all who received him, to those who believed in his name, he gave the right to become children of God—children born not of natural descent, nor of human decision or a husband's will, but born of God.

This is the first intimation in John's Gospel of the doctrine of the new birth which is characteristic of both the Gospel and the First Letter of John.

John's teaching, like Paul's, is that Christ is received by faith (Col. 2:6–7). What John adds to Paul's outline is that faith brings the privilege of adoption, and paradoxically, that same faith is the fruit of a birth which comes from God! Those who receive Christ and enter into adoption are those who have been born 'not of natural descent, *nor of human decision* or a husband's will, but born of God'. A rather similar emphasis can be noted in our Lord's words to Nicodemus, where Jesus emphasises that without a new birth no man can either see or enter the kingdom of God (Jn. 3:3, 5). The new life, which Paul has taught us leads from God's plan begun before time to its consummation after time has ended, is now expanded by John. He indicates that our personal experience of it begins when God touches our lives in his wonderful power, in regeneration.

We can now see the wide range of doctrines which go to make up the doctrine of the Christian life. The eternal choice of God's love in election touches our lives in his *calling*. He gives the *new birth* which enables us to enter the kingdom of God by *faith* and *repentance*. When we believe and repent, God *justifies* us. *Adoption* is a further gift, so that as assured children we may live lives of *sanctification* until the day of our *glorification* comes. In general terms this is the plan of salvation. It is also the order in which we will study these individual doctrines.

In Christ

It is in Christ we receive all the blessings of the Christian life. We are chosen in him. In him we are predestined to be like him. In Christ we are called, and in him born again to newness of life (1 Pet. 1:3). In him we have faith, and receive the Holy Spirit. In him we are brought into the privileges of brotherhood in the family of God. In Christ is our sanctification (1 Cor. 1:30). When we see him, we will be made like him, for when he appears in glory, we shall also appear with Christ (1 Jn. 3:2; Col. 3:4). From beginning to end all blessings are ours in Christ.

PRACTICAL REPERCUSSIONS

We have already tried to indicate that this analysis is more than a mere academic exercise. It is intended to enlarge our appreciation of what has become of us since Christ began to master our lives. We will see more fully as we follow the details of this pattern that an increased sense of what it means to be a Christian should always strengthen in our lives the chief marks of being a Christian.

This should lead us to a deeper *humility*. Humility is not simply feeling small and useless—like an inferiority complex. It is sensing how great and glorious God is, and seeing myself in that light. Humility in Scripture is the fruit of grace, not of fear. It is God's *love* which makes a man truly humble. Now, Scripture emphasises these aspects of the Christian life to show us the depth and length, the breadth and height of the love of God. When we see *that* we are humbled by the knowledge that God cares so much about us.

This should lead us *to a steadier assurance*. Lack of assurance is often caused, like a sense of inferiority, by being too taken up with ourselves. But our assurance does not lie in what we are, be we great or small. It lies in what God has done in his plan of salvation to secure us to himself. 'Believe God's word and power more than you believe your own feelings and experiences,' wrote Samuel Rutherford to a correspondent. 'Your Rock is Christ, and it is not the Rock which ebbs and flows, but your sea.' The more we know of the strength of our Rock, and understand that we have all the blessings of the Christian life secure in him, the more steadily assured we will be and the greater will be our joy.

Understanding the plan of salvation also leads us *to worship*. Is this not the final meaning of Romans 8 and Ephesians 1? We may praise God in defiance of all enemies. We may bless God, that is, literally 'speak well' of him, and find loving him to be our greatest delight and serving him to be the most satisfying thing in the world.

> *To the Name of our Salvation*
> *Laud and honour let us pay,*
> *Which for many a generation*
> *Hid in God's foreknowledge lay,*
> *But with holy exultation*
> *We may sing aloud today.*
>
> *Jesus is the Name exalted*
> *Over every other name;*
> *In this Name, whene'er assaulted,*
> *We can put our foes to shame;*
> *Strength to them who else had halted,*
> *Eyes to blind, and feet to lame.*
>
> *Therefore we, in love adoring,*
> *This most blessed Name revere,*
> *Holy Jesus, Thee imploring*
> *So to write it in us here*
> *That hereafter, heavenward souring,*
> *We may sing with angels there.*

How this plan of salvation begins to touch our lives is the first thing we must consider. We become Christians because we have heard Christ calling us to follow him. What this means in detail is the subject of our next chapter.

4
Called by God

When *Onward Christian soldiers* describes the church as 'Chosen, called and faithful' it introduces a subtle change into the Bible's words. The book of Revelation has a different order. There Christians are 'called, chosen and faithful' (Rev. 17:14). Does this mean Scripture teaches that men are called and *then* chosen? In the light of the passages in Romans and Ephesians discussed in the previous chapter this can hardly be so. None the less, a good case can be made out in the study of Christian truth for giving attention to the doctrine of *calling*, or vocation before considering in any detail the more sensitive areas of biblical teaching which include election and predestination.

The reason for doing this is not merely to postpone controversy until towards the end of the book! Many Christians are surprised to discover that John Calvin (the Reformer whose name is linked inextricably with the doctrine of predestination) often wrestled with the problem of where to fit the doctrine of election. In his greatest work, *The Institutes of the Christian Religion*, he eventually placed it at the end of his exposition of the Christian life! This is a very different place from its more logical position (as for example in the Westminster Confession) at the beginning of a system of doctrine. But Calvin's final resting place for the doctrine is very similar to its position in Romans. In terms of Ephesians of course, we find solid biblical precedent for treating election at the beginning of theology. In a sense Scripture does both.

One thing can be said which perhaps tips the balances in favour of our leaving predestination to a later point in our study. It is that when a doctrine has become a matter of controversy Christians frequently fail to think about it in the context of the whole of Scripture and also of the other doctrines which are closely related to it. In the case of election it is difficult to the point of impossibility to grasp its real meaning without having a general appreciation of the whole character of the Christian life. For these reasons we will by-pass it for the moment, and return to it when the general direction of the rest of biblical teaching has become clear. In this chapter we will take up the study of *Divine Calling.*

THE CALL OF GOD

We became Christians because God called us. Peter tells us:

> But you are a chosen people, a royal priesthood, a holy nation, a people belonging to God, that you may declare the praises of him who called you out of darkness into his marvellous light.
>
> 1 Peter 2:9

The same picture is often used in the pages of the New Testament.

Our Lord Jesus Christ's summons to men and women to enter the kingdom of God is sometimes spoken of as a 'call'. 'I have not come to call the righteous, but sinners' (Matt. 9:13). He does not mean to imply that his summons addresses itself to only a section of mankind, since all men stand under the call to repent and believe the gospel; but the call of Christ 'locks in' to the hearts of men who are aware of their sinfulness and need. It is such men who 'hear' the voice of Christ summoning them. Others are deaf to his overtures. John records a similar idea in the picture of Christ as the Good Shepherd:

> The man who enters by the gate is the shepherd of the sheep. The watchman opens the gate for him, and the sheep listen to his voice. He calls his own sheep by name and leads them out. When he has brought out all his own he goes on ahead of them, and his sheep follow him because they know his voice. But they will never follow a stranger; in fact they will run away from him because they do not recognise a stranger's voice.
>
> John 10:2-5

Those who heard Jesus on that occasion did not understand what he meant. But his meaning should not be difficult to grasp. He is describing in picture-language what it means to become a Christian. Few things are more awe-inspiring than the first occasions when we become conscious that Another is addressing us. For many people the first sense of it is when they hear a sermon, or read a book or some portion of the Bible, and discover that it seems to speak directly to their personal circumstances. Preachers are occasionally accused of exposing the lives of their hearers when they have known nothing about the person who has been so disturbed. The sharp, personal edge of God's word has touched them! Slowly it dawns, as the Speaker emerges from the voice of the messenger, that the voice we heard was the voice of the Shepherd; he has been calling us by name, and now we recognise his accent as he draws us into his flock and we become his lambs. Thereafter we look to hear his unmistakable commands throughout the whole of our lives (Jn. 10:27).

So much for our experience of the call of Christ. But the biblical teaching on Calling is a wider and deeper theme than we have yet indicated.

Old Testament Background

In the Old Testament the verb *qara* signifies both to name (e.g. Gen. 1:5, 8, 10) and to summon (e.g. Gen. 3:9). Throughout the Old Testament these two meanings exist side by side. But in the prophetic writings particularly, the call of God is seen as a command to listen to his voice and walk in obedience to it. In this the prophets are basically summoning the people back to their allegiance to God in the Covenant. They often refer to God's covenant message to Israel recorded in Deuteronomy 26:16–31:13. But as the prophets reflect on that Covenant which God had forged with his people at Sinai, they become conscious of a new pressure on their spirits. Because of the disobedience of the people, another emphasis begins to emerge. They see that God had done more than call his people *in the sense of speaking to them*. It was his calling which had *created them in the first place*. Just as his voice had called the universe into being, so he had called into being a people who would be a fit reflection of his love and glory. He called Israel by name. She is his (Is. 43:12). 'When Israel was a child', says God, 'I loved him, and out of Egypt I *called* my son' (Hos. 11:1). God's call was not only a summons, but it seemed to display a creative power. Alongside this emphasis we discover something rather puzzling. God also issues a call which does not seem to be answered. Isaiah reserves some of his most anguished words to describe the poignancy of this situation:

> I will destine you for the sword,
> and you will all bend down for the slaughter;
> *for I called but you did not answer.*
> I spoke but you did not listen . . .
>
> I also will choose harsh treatment for them
> and will bring upon them what they dread.
> *For when I called, no-one answered,*
> when I spoke, no-one listened.
> They did evil in my sight
> and chose what displeases me.
>
> Isaiah 65:12; 66:4

Jeremiah apparently bore the same burden upon his sensitive prophetic spirit:

> While you were doing all these things, declares the Lord, I spoke to you again, but you did not listen; *I called you, but you did not answer* . . .
>
> So do not pray for this people nor offer any plea or petition for them; do not plead with me, for I will not listen to you.
>
> Therefore, this is what the Lord God Almighty, the God of Israel, says: 'Listen! I am going to bring on Judah and on everyone living in Jerusalem every disaster I pronounced against them. I spoke to them, but they did not listen; *I called to them, but they did not answer.*'
>
> Jeremiah 7:13, 16; 35:17

There is a strange ambiguity here. On the one hand, God's call seems to have its own creative power. On the other hand, God opens his arms and his heart to the rebellious as he calls them, but his summons seems to fall empty to the ground and meet with no positive response. It is irresistible, and yet it seems to be rejectable!

In the New Testament this same ambiguity persists. Jesus says that many are called but few are chosen (Matt. 22:14). Here there seems to be a contrast between the larger number who receive the call and the smaller number who respond positively to it. By contrast in Paul's letters, God's 'call' is almost invariably seen as powerful and effective.

These two apparently different kinds of calling are often described by the terms *General Call* and *Effectual Call*. What are the patterns of thought which lie behind this distinction?

GENERAL CALLING

God summons men to acknowledge him. He 'speaks' through creation and providence. Psalm 19 reflects the Old Testament consciousness of this:

> The heavens declare the glory of God;
>   the skies proclaim the work of his hands.
> Day after day they pour forth speech;
>   night after night they display knowledge.
> There is no speech or language
>   where their voice is not heard.
> Their voice goes out into all the earth,
>   their words to the ends of the world.
>
>   Psalm 19:1–4

This is not meant to be an argument for the existence of God. Certainly it would be stretching Scripture to turn this into a primitive form of the argument from design! The Psalm presupposes that God has revealed himself in history to his people the Jews. But, on that basis, he declares that the same God who reveals himself in acts and words is the God whose autograph is written in the heavens. The call to all men which declares God's being, his glory and his handiwork, rises above the barriers of language and culture. God's revelation of his character presses in upon all men, everywhere, all of the time. Paul speaks about this in Romans 1:20. God's eternal power and deity are clearly inscribed on all he has made. Man's own being, distorted as it is by the Fall, is a testimony to God, and fragments of God's law written in the heart at creation continue to shine through spasmodically (Rom. 2:12–16).

In addition to this general revelation of God to mankind, the word of the Cross is also to be preached to all men. It is the duty of the Christian church in every age and place to proclaim to every person that there is provision for his needs in Christ.

The first disciples were to obey and transmit the command of the Master: Go into all the world and preach the good news to all creation. Whoever believes and is baptised will be saved, but whoever does not believe will be condemned. This invitation to salvation is given in the gospel of Christ (cf. Acts 2:31; 17:30; Matt. 11:28-30). But clearly it is not always received. Many are called, but the 'chosen' are few. In fact, instead of softening hearts and drawing men to Christ, the preaching of his message may result in a hardening which is increased by rejecting the grace which is offered in the good news. For both Old and New Testament prophets this was one of the inexplicable realities of their ministry. Here Isaiah and Jesus were one (cf. Is. 6:9-10; Mk. 4:12).

But it is clear that the same language is used in Scripture to describe a call which has very different results.

Effectual Calling

One of the New Testament's most frequent one-word descriptions of the Christian is that he is 'called'. The believers in Rome (Rom. 1:6, 7); Corinth, (1 Cor. 1:2); Galatia (Gal. 1:6), Ephesus (Eph. 4:1, 4); Philippi (Phil. 3:14-15); Colosse (Col. 3:15); Thessalonica (2 Thess. 1:11), are all 'called ones', and in each case it is obvious that God's summons achieved its purpose. It is clearly in this sense that Paul uses the term in the great chain of saving acts in Romans 8:28. Can we find some resolution to the tension which exists between these two dimensions? Are there two different calls issued by God? Perhaps the simplest solution is also the best. There is a call which comes to all men from God through the many evidences he has left of his presence in the world. But there are also times when God sends notices of demand, as it were, rather than reminders: when he comes personally, knocking at the door, rather than by circular letter!

Of course, there is an element of mystery in this experience. We know what it is to hear God addressing us powerfully and personally, through a passage in the Bible, or a sermon we hear. But when we discuss the passage or sermon with others we discover that it has cut little ice with them. We may not be able to say why God has spoken in this clear way to us and not to others. We only know that in his sovereign wisdom he has. We know that two people can listen to the same evangelistic sermon and one will hear the voice of Christ calling him to faith while the other hears only the words of the preacher. Again, we do not know why this happens. We are at a loss to fathom the difference between a general call and this powerful, effectual call. We only know that the difference is real.

Looked at from this point of view there are a number of important things to notice.

(i) Called by God the Father

There are many verses in the New Testament which indicate that the source of our invitation to become Christians lies in the Father. This has more practical relevance than we might ordinarily notice. It implies that the Father lovingly invites us to himself. If we grasp this, we will be delivered from a deep-seated suspicion of God which continues to haunt many Christians. Sometimes in the past the gospel has been presented in such a way as to give a distorted view of God, as though the Father consented unwillingly and rather grudgingly to the salvation of men, only because of the insistent demands of his loving Son. But verses like Romans 1:6–7; 8:28, 1 Corinthians 1:2, 24; Hebrews 9:15; Jude 1, all indicate that God as the Father of Jesus Christ, is the Great Inviter. He loves us, calls us, saves us just as surely as does our Lord Jesus Christ. Many youngsters know what it is to have their father call them from play, and to trudge home, wet, late and dirty, to his impending wrath! We, by contrast are summoned by God the Father not to receive a row but his open-armed embrace!

(ii) Called in the power of the Spirit

God's call is a demonstration of his mighty power. That sense of the divine authority runs through Paul's words in Romans 8:30 with their steady beat of the footsteps of a God who accomplishes his purposes. In the power of the Spirit, *we are called out of darkness into light.* (1 Pet. 2:9), and delivered from the kingdom and reign of the powers of darkness (Col 1:13). *We are also called out of death and into life,* as our Lord indicates: the time has already come when the (spiritually) dead hear his voice (Jn. 5:25). Here the great paradox of calling is vividly illustrated, for how can dead men hear? But he who calls them creates in them the ability to respond so that in the very act of his calling he brings them into new life. The best illustration of this occurs later on in John's Gospel, in the raising of Lazarus. How could a dead man respond to Jesus' voice? There is something quite beyond our understanding in this miracle. But the experience of Lazarus pictorialises for us what happens spiritually when we are brought into the kingdom of God and given a new life. *We are called out of bondage and into freedom.* Formerly we were slaves of sin (Eph. 2:3), but now Christ has set us free for his service. Paul associates Christian freedom with the call of God in Galatians 5:13: 'You, my brothers, were called to be free.' So, says Jesus, 'If the Son sets you free, you will be free indeed' (Jn. 8:36).

(iii) Called by grace to holiness and heaven

God's call is *gracious* in the sense that it shows us the graciousness of God. But it is also gracious in the sense that it is totally unmerited, indeed ill-deserved on our part. To be called is to be the recipient of grace (2 Tim. 1:9). Remember Paul's powerful rhetoric to the Corinthians when he argues out this point—God has not called many of the 'greats' of this world but set his divine invitation on the poor and lowly as though to indicate that his call to men is drawn out from him by nothing but his own love and favour to sinners (1 Cor. 1:26-9).

God's call is *holy*. We are 'called saints'. Of course we are called *to be* saints, but Paul undoubtedly means something more when he uses this expression. It is the calling of God that separates us for God, that sanctifies us. To stand under that call is therefore to be given up to a life of holiness and to be locked in to the pathway of obedience which leads to his heavenly kingdom. It is important to notice that the very character of our calling is a determining factor in our witness. We are called to live in such a way that the praise of God may be seen (1 Pet. 2:9) and called to suffer with Christ in imitation of his life (1 Pet. 2:21).

As far as its direction is concerned the divine call is *heavenly*. We share in a heavenly calling (Heb. 3:1), and this is 'the hope to which he has called you' (Eph. 1:18) in which we have already begun to share here and now (cf. Eph. 4:4). We are called to God's kingdom and glory (2 Thess. 2:14) and are given the assurance that 'the God of all grace who called you to his eternal glory in Christ ... will himself ... make you strong, firm and steadfast' (1 Pet. 5:10). It is clear then that God's calling is something which both inaugurates the Christian life and determines the shape of it at every stage in its development.

IMPLICATIONS

What then are the *implications* of God's call? In the first place it clearly emphasises that the initiative in spiritual experience is God's, and not man's. We have neither claim nor right to his gracious summons, any more than the unformed mass of darkness and chaos in the primeval time could lay claim to the voice of God to bring light and form order. It is this same God who said, 'Let light shine out of darkness', who has shone into our hearts to give us the light of the knowledge of the glory of God in the face of Christ (2 Cor. 4:6).

Secondly, calling bears fruit in moral conformity. We must live lives which are worthy of our calling, expressing a lifestyle which is consistent with the originating grace of our pilgrimage. The beam that shines upon us from Zion's hill sets before us a sometimes narrow way as it leads us to life. But that heavenly spotlight, however increasingly narrow its beam appears to men in spiritual darkness, leads us nearer and nearer to our Eternal Source. We shall discover the closer we get to that Source the more intense and glorious does the revelation of God's infinite grace appear. In this Simon Peter, who had once shrunk from the implications of his call, and hidden tearfully from men in the darkness of the Jerusalem night, was later able to rejoice as he saw that he too had been called out of the darkness into God's *marvellous* light! (1 Pet. 2:9).

Thirdly, God's calling has this implication: it requires confirmation in our lives. Peter again urges us to make our calling and election secure (2 Pet 1:10). The only way to identify the voice, to reassure ourselves that we truly heard it, is Samuel-like to respond: 'Speak, for your servant is listening' (1 Sam. 3:10). Obedience is the test of our spiritual hearing.

*'Tis Jesus calls me on
To perfect faith and love,
To perfect hope and peace and trust,
For earth and heaven above.*

*'Tis Jesus who confirms
The blessed work within,
By adding grace to welcomed grace,
Where reigned the power of sin.*
Lewis Hartsough

But before this peace is experienced, we may discover that God *disturbs* us.

5
Conviction of Sin

There is a major danger attached to formulating a doctrine of Christian experience. It is the tendency to give the impression that experience which may take time fully to develop is consummated in an instant. This is easily done with the theme of divine calling. The very expression lends itself to the idea of an instantaneous and short-lived summons. But when we see the idea of vocation in the light of the rest of biblical teaching and when it is illustrated in personal experience, effectual calling is seen to be something which often extends over a period of time. It is also true that in the history of the church effectual calling has at times been regarded as synonymous with regeneration. Consequently it has been thought of as a sudden work of God. Perhaps this is where the old idea of 'awakening' helps us to grasp the picture more clearly. Someone rouses us out of a deep slumber, and their voice penetrates our subconscious. We stir within, and then become aware of a distant disturbance. We fight against it, seeking the tranquillity of sleep—but it has penetrated our senses. Gradually we become aware of ourselves, of our circumstances, and eventually of the identity of the one who has called us. For many people a religious 'awakening' is exactly like this. It can be a profoundly disturbing experience.

As a young boy, when capital punishment was still administered in the United Kingdom, I used to waken with a sense of horror on the rare morning when an execution was to take place. What could it be like to be roused that morning from fitful slumber to realise one's identity as a condemned prisoner and to remember that *this* was the day appointed for life to end? Now, awakening—that inward spiritual process which is the result of God's call—brings to the surface a similar sense of the reality of our condition before God. It makes us aware of his condemning judgment upon our sin unless we can find some means of salvation.

This is what our Lord described in the parable of the Prodigal Son, or the Waiting Father. In the far country the reckless youngster in his need heard the echoes of home sounding in the depths of his subconscious. He 'came to himself' (Lk. 15:17 R.S.V.), and then returned to his father. Something very similar took place in the life of Saul of Tarsus. He thought all was well with him. Indeed in comparison with his contemporaries his position before God seemed secure (Phil. 3:6). Then God began to speak to him through his word, piercing into his heart by the inward application of the Law (Rom. 7:6–13). Saul kicked against the goads of conviction (Acts 26:14). But now he was awakened to his spiritual need, was sovereignly confronted by Christ on the road to Damascus and called into the kingdom. He experienced what has been called 'the breaking up of the insensibility of the sinner'. *In plain terms he was convicted of sin.*

We ought to give much more attention to this aspect of spiritual experience than we do. It is intimately related to the character of the whole of our Christian lives. Its neglect has left the quality of Christian living of our day relatively poorer, for grace often grows strongest where conviction of sin has pierced deepest. This was the perspective of Jesus: those who are most conscious of what has been forgiven are those most likely to love much (cf. Lk. 7:36–50). But those who are most conscious of forgiveness are invariably those who have been most acutely convicted of their sin.

The Author of Conviction

Jesus promised that he would send the Holy Spirit to 'convict the world of guilt in regard to sin and righteousness and judgment' (Jn. 16:8). The word John uses for 'convict' means 'to scorn', 'to pour contempt' and 'to convince'. It is this severe ministry which the Holy Spirit exercises in his office as Advocate. It is in his work of glorifying Christ and vindicating him that, of necessity, the Spirit must accomplish this painful work in men's hearts. He defends Christ and vindicates him; but in so doing he serves as the counsel for the prosecution in God's indictment against sinners.

It is important for a proper understanding of Jesus' words to recognise that in the context of his message the primary reference of these words is to the Day of Pentecost. For the Spirit will convict 'in regard to sin and righteousness and judgment' only 'when he comes' (Jn. 16:8). The whole thrust of our Lord's sermon indicates that the Spirit will come after Christ's death and resurrection, and upon his ascension and return to the right hand of the Father (14:26; 15:26; 16:7). The day 'when he comes' (15:26; 16:8) is clearly the Day of Pentecost (cf. Acts 1:8; 2:1). If we examine the prophecy of Jesus in the light of its particular fulfilment on that day, we should also be able to uncover the groundplan of this ministry of the Spirit in every age.

Conviction by the Spirit takes place in three areas; *Sin, Righteousness* and *Judgment*.

Conviction of sin is produced because men do not believe in Christ (Jn. 16:9). This does not mean that men are sinners because they do not believe. It is sometimes mistakenly said that since Christ's coming the only sin is that of unbelief and faithlessness will be the only ground of condemnation. But this is not at all what our Lord means. His teaching is that *men do not believe because they are sinners*. The apex of their sin is unbelief in the face of the full light of divine revelation. What therefore takes place when the Spirit of God comes upon a man's life, awakening him, is the realisation of his guilt before God, the fact that he has no resources to meet God's charge and no Saviour in whom to hide from God's wrath (for he does not believe in Christ). He is Christ-less and hope-less (Eph. 2:12).

Conviction of righteousness is produced because Christ goes to the Father (Jn. 16:10). It would be possible to understand these words in isolation as referring to the sense awakened in the hearts of the convicted that they lack righteousness, and that this is what Christ supplies. But that does not clarify the whole statement, nor does it take account of the emphasis on the Spirit's work *in directing attention to the Lord Jesus Christ*.

The words 'because I am going to the Father' provide us with a clue to interpretation. Christ goes to the Father, in John's terminology, by death, resurrection and ascension (cf. 14:12, 28; 16:28). It is to these events that the Spirit will bear witness because they provide the divine vindication of Christ. They show that God has justified his Son in the face of man's rejection of him. It seems to be to this that Paul alludes in 1 Timothy 3:16, when he says that Christ was 'vindicated by the Spirit' (perhaps primarily in the resurrection, Rom. 1:4). When the Spirit displays Christ's righteousness, he thereby displays man's guilt, and thus brings an abiding sense of conviction as a consequence.

Conviction of judgment is produced because the prince of this world is judged (Jn. 16:11). Men laughingly despise the notion of a judgment to come, and they do so because they have been blinded by Satan (2 Cor. 4:4). But on the Cross Christ conquered and judged the prince of this world and made an open show of him in his triumph (Jn. 12:32; Col. 2:15–16). If *he* is condemned, *he* the leader of the Christless, the judgment and condemnation of men is even more certain. The death of Christ, which unbelieving men took to be the judgment of God on him was in fact the judgment of their master, and therefore a guarantee of their own impending doom!

The ministry of the Spirit thus produces a total reversal, a conversion in our thinking. Instead of calling Christ in question we discover that we are being called in question by his Spirit. The contempt or indifference or opposition which we poured upon him now rebounds upon us. The positions are reversed: It is not Christ who on the Cross is declared guilty of sin—but *I am declared guilty*!
It is not Christ who is condemned—but *I who am condemned*!

This interpretation is borne out by the fulfilment of these prophetic words on the Day of Pentecost. When the Spirit came and in the preaching of Peter the Lord Jesus Christ was proclaimed and exalted, three things resulted:

(i) men were impressed by the fact of their unbelief (Acts 2:23; 36).
(ii) they were persuaded of the righteousness and vindication of Christ (Acts 2:24; 32:33).
(iii) they recognised his exaltation as Lord over all his enemies (Acts 2:34–6).

The immediate result of this was deeply-felt conviction: 'When the people heard this, they were cut to the heart and said to Peter and the other apostles, "Brothers, what shall we do?"' (Acts 2:37). These are the words of men who have been convicted of sin. The prophecy of Jesus had been fulfilled.

Evangelical Christianity has generally held that this Pentecostal conviction of sin was not the only fulfilment of Christ's promise. It has been argued that in this respect Pentecost simply writes in capital letters what it always means to become a Christian. The experiences of men like Martin Luther and John Bunyan spring to mind as illustrations.

In more recent times, however, questions have been raised about the validity of these assumptions. Today, generally speaking, the necessity of conviction as a forerunner of commitment to Christ is rarely emphasised, and may even be denied. There are three questions we must therefore consider.

QUESTIONS ABOUT CONVICTION

(i) *Is* conviction necessary?

Undoubtedly some people become Christians without an agonising sense of conviction of personal guilt. For example there are Christians who know nothing of the radical upheaval in which others' first experience of Christ and salvation began. There are also those who apparently come to Christ in adolescence or maturer years with little of the signs of battle which others know. It is vital that we should recognise this lest we stereotype the operations of God's Spirit without biblical warrant. This is precisely why Paul emphasises that there are 'different kinds of working, but the same God works all of them in all men' (1 Cor. 12:6). C. H. Spurgeon expressed the balance to which he had come like this:

> Among the many thousands of souls who have been brought to know the Lord under my instrumentality, I have often noticed that a considerable proportion of these, and of the best members of our church too, were won to the Saviour by gentler means ... I asked an excellent young woman, 'What was the first thought that set you really seeking the Saviour?' 'Oh, Sir,' she replied, 'It was Christ's lovely character that first made me long to be his disciple. I saw how kind, how good, how disinterested, how self-sacrificing he was, and that made me feel how different I was. I thought "Oh, I am not like Jesus", and that sent me to my room, and I began to pray, and so I came to trust him.'
>
> *The Full Harvest*, p. 235

These words are illuminating for several reasons. They indicate that we should look twice at Scripture before raising the experience of Paul, for example, into the sole prototype of conversion. The events of the Day of Pentecost are not the norm for all forthcoming experiences of repentance and faith. But Spurgeon's words are also significant because they show that even when God uses 'gentler means' to bring us to Christ, there is always (at least in those who have reached natural maturity), some sense of the conviction of sin. 'Oh, I am not like Jesus' is an expression of such conviction. It is difficult to see how this, or something akin to it, can be avoided if we are to be awakened out of our slumber in sin and transferred to the kingdom of God.

We need to learn that conviction is not something which we ourselves create. The fears and anxieties which often accompany it are not duties to be fulfilled if we are to become genuine Christians. It is a great mistake to be impressed by the depth of conviction of a Bunyan and to seek the same for oneself. God does not deal with us like that. The Puritan writer John Owen well expresses a healthier attitude:

> God is pleased to exercise a prerogative and sovereignty in this whole matter, and deals with the souls of men in unspeakable variety. Some he leads by the gates of death and hell unto rest in his love ... and the paths of others he makes plain and easy unto them.
>
> *Works* III:360

(ii) How much conviction is necessary?

The best answer is: whatever depth and length of conviction will draw us to faith in Christ. Degrees of conviction will differ just as believers do themselves. It is impossible to offer a general prescription, or even to judge in advance the operations of the Holy Spirit. Again we have to reach back into the literature of previous centuries to find help in these crucial pastoral areas, and in this instance to the vigorous words of another Puritan, Thomas Watson:

> God does not prescribe an exact proportion of sorrow and humiliation. A knotty piece of timber requires more wedges to be driven into it. Some stomachs are fouler than others,

therefore need stronger physic [medicine]. But wouldest thou know when thou hast been humbled enough for sin? When thou art willing to let go thy sins. The gold has lain long enough in the furnace when the dross is purged out; so, when the love of sin is purged out, a soul is humbled enough for divine acceptance, though not for divine satisfaction. Now, if thou art humbled enough, what needs more? If a needle will let out the imposthume [abscess], what needs a lance? Be not more cruel to thyself than God would have thee.

A Body of Divinity (1890), p. 451

(iii) What is the purpose of conviction?

The Spirit convicts us of sin in order to bring us to Christ. Conviction of sin is the process by which we gain a proper perspective on our lives in the sight of God so that we may cast ourselves upon his grace and mercy in the Cross. It follows inevitably that conviction enhances Christian character in two ways:

(a) *It produces humility*. When Paul argues sinful man to silence in Romans 1 : 18–3 : 20 he creates this kind of humility. Every man's mouth is stopped and the whole world becomes conscious of its guilt. That leaves a lasting impression in a person's life. To be silenced before the throne of God is an unforgettable experience! It shows every time we speak with and to others.

(b) *It produces thankfulness*. It is in proportion to our sense of need that we are able to grasp the measure of God's grace. The more aware we become of our personal condition, through conviction, the more remarkable does the love of God for us seem to be. Thankfulness grows best in the seed-bed of conviction, just as some plants must be placed in the soil in the winter if they are to flower in the summer.

The circumstances which surround our entry into the kingdom of God are as significant in the world of the spirit as the circumstances surrounding our natural birth can be to the rest of our lives. Because God sees what he intends to produce in us and through us as his children he exposes us to differing levels of conviction. Some, like the hearers of Peter's sermon on Pentecost, are under conviction for minutes; others, like Paul, perhaps for days; yet others go through a dark night of the soul which seems interminable, like Bunyan and Luther before him. These differences lie in the hands of God. What lies in our hands is that, with whatever measure of conviction our hearts are filled, we should come to Christ and trust him wholly and only as our Saviour. Thus, as we become increasingly conscious of our need of him, we will learn to live out before the eye of God lives of whole-hearted thankful obedience to him.

> *From depths of woe I raise to Thee*
> *The voice of lamentation;*
> *Lord, turn a gracious ear to me*
> *And hear my supplication.*
> *If Thou shouldst be extreme to mark*
> *Each secret sin and misdeed dark,*
> *O who could stand before Thee?*
>
> *Although our sin is great indeed,*
> *God's mercies far exceed it;*
> *His hand can give the help we need,*
> *However much we need it:*
> *He is the Shepherd of the sheep*
> *Who Israel doth guard and keep*
> *And shall from sin redeem him.*
>
> Martin Luther.
> Translated by Richard Massie

6
Born Again

Thus far we have given attention to what are essentially preliminary features of the Christian life. We have moved from a brief summary of our need of God's saving grace to the plan of God which lies behind the whole of our experience of it. We have also thought about the call and summons of God which awakens us from our natural slumber and indifference in sin, brings conviction of our guilty condition before God, and leads us into the hallway of salvation itself.

We are now at the point in our study where perhaps the most crucial doctrine of all must be examined. That doctrine is Regeneration. To have clear views here is to pave the way for all the other doctrines of the Christian life; to mistake the way here, conversely, will mean that the whole focus of our understanding is seriously at fault.

REGENERATION AND THE GOSPEL

Evangelism, like so many other things in life, tends to pass through phases. Sometimes its emphasis centres on *the necessity* of 'regeneration', 'the new birth' or being 'born again'.

I vividly and rather painfully remember being asked once in my teens whether I were a Christian. On replying 'yes' I was further asked if I were a 'true Christian'. Once more I replied 'yes, I hope so!' only to be asked yet again in a tone of mild exasperation (on the suspicion that these first two answers were unlikely to be true!) was I a 'born-again' Christian? At that time it was common for people to insist in both preaching and personal witnessing that 'you must be born again'.

In many ways it may be a good thing that one encounters this less and less as the heart of evangelism. For one thing 'you must be born again' is not in itself good news! For another it is nowhere in the New Testament suggested that this is the heart of the gospel or the object of faith. Paul apparently did not cross the ancient world with this emphasis on his lips. His message was of Christ crucified, risen and exalted to whom men should turn in faith and repentance.

It is therefore not surprising that, in reaction to this very evangelistic emphasis, it has frequently been said that the New Testament has virtually nothing to say about regeneration. The word is used on only two occasions in Scripture, according to the A.V. (King James version). In other versions 'rebirth' or 'regeneration' may appear only once. In Matthew 19:28 it refers to the renewal of all things in the last days, the new heavens and the new earth; in Titus 3:5 it refers either to the personal experience of new life, or to the symbol of it in baptism. This is meagre evidence on which to build what has already been described as 'perhaps the most crucial doctrine of all'!

Yet, granted these concessions, the doctrine of regeneration cannot be so easily dismissed. Other passages of Scripture employ similar ideas, and yet more passages illustrate the same idea by different metaphors, analogies and illustrations. But before examining these a word must be said about the expression 'regeneration' itself.

In some traditions it has been tied very closely to the doctrine of baptism, through verses like John 3:5; Ephesians 5:26; Titus 3:5, baptism bringing regeneration and 'regeneration' being used virtually as a synonym for baptism. With due respect for the integrity of those who have held this view, it fails to take account of the context in which the idea of new life appears. It cannot be consistently upheld in passages where the idea of regeneration is expressed in quite different language in contexts where there is no possible reference to baptism.

At the opposite extreme, in some evangelical traditions, 'you must be born again' is regarded virtually as the equivalent of a command to believe in Christ. It is something we must do. But in the New Testament new birth is something God gives. The point of the metaphor lies in the fact that the new birth is *not* something we can do.

Sometimes, 'regeneration' is taken to mean the whole process of becoming a Christian, and is understood as a comparatively broadly-based term.

We will take 'regeneration' to refer to the fundamental imparting of new life by God which lies at the heart of being a

Christian, the first abiding of the seed of God in our lives, as the first letter of John describes it.

Pictures of Regeneration

The word 'regeneration' means 'another Genesis'. It is expounded in the pages of the New Testament under three images:

(i) Birth

Becoming a Christian, receiving Christ, begins according to John 1:12, by being born of the will of God. Later in the same Gospel Jesus says that it is the indispensable requirement to seeing and entering the kingdom of God (Jn. 3:3, 5). It is a current which runs through 1 John—Christians are defined as those who are born of God (cf. 1 Jn. 2:29; 3:9; 4:7; 5:1, 4). But the *idea* of birth is not exclusive to John's writings. James speaks of God bringing us forth by the word of truth, to be a kind of first-fruits of his creatures (Jas. 1:18). He uses a medical term for the end of a pregnancy. 1 Peter speaks twice about believers being the recipients of a 'new birth' (1 Pet. 1:3, 23). Elsewhere the same kind of language is employed—Christians may be 'newborn babies', they are to grow to full maturity (Col. 1:28; Eph. 4:13–17). Those with a pastoral responsibility travail over their spiritual children (Gal. 4:19—'My little children, for whom I am again in the pains of childbirth until Christ is formed in you').

(ii) Creation

The second word picture is one which draws a parallel between what God did at the beginning of time and the miracle of his grace which brings us into the 'new time' or 'new age' which we enter through Christ. It may well be that we are to see the merging of these two ideas in the New Testament's word for regeneration—'a second Genesis'. The picture is a very dramatic one. Paul employs it when he is at the height of his powers of vivid and imaginative insight into God's work within us. In a moment of great spiritual tension at the end of his letter to the Galatians, he affirms that the only thing that really matters is 'a new creation' (Gal. 6:15). Without this everything is in vain. Again, later in his ministry the same imagery is employed at much greater length: the light which shines into the darkness of our hearts, bringing us into the presence of God can only be paralleled by two events in the history of the world—the creation at the beginning, and the resurrection of Christ as the harbinger of the world to come (2 Cor. 4:6–12). Later in the same section of his letter he makes the glorious statement that to be in Christ is to share already in that world which is yet to be. Literally his words are: 'if anyone in Christ—new creation!' (2 Cor. 5:17). Here, as elsewhere, Paul's great purpose is to draw attention to the magnitude of what God has already done in our little lives by his grace. If only we would allow this to expand our minds, and so enter into the enjoyment of these great privileges, we would see something of the glory of God exhibited in the character and quality of our living!

(iii) Resurrection

We have hinted already that the new birth can be paralleled to life being brought forth out of nothing in creation, but also at the even more amazing truth which thrilled Paul: greater yet than life and order out of emptiness and chaos is life out of its opposite, death! This indicates the extent of God's work in us and also hints at its source in the resurrection of Jesus. So Paul argues in Romans 6:13 that, since we are united to a risen Christ and therefore share in his risen power, we should live as 'dead men brought to life'. When we were dead through sin, God reached down *in* Christ to resurrect us *with* Christ by his grace (Eph. 2:5). The Christian has 'passed from death to life' (1 Jn. 3:14)!

What is being underscored in all these passages is that regeneration, however it is described, is a divine activity in us, in which we are not the actors but the recipients. As well to tell a lame man to walk, a blind man to see, as to tell a dead man to live, a man without spiritual life to have it, or to say 'you must be born again'! There is a paradox in the gospel at this point. For wwe discover that the one thing needful is almost the only thing outside our power to perform. This disturbing thought must be considered further.

WHY IS REGENERATION NECESSARY?

The terminology of regeneration is largely gathered from the writings of the apostle John, and the *locus classicus* of its exposition is found of course in Jesus' discussion with Nicodemus recorded in John 3. There our Lord says to the great Teacher of Israel, 'It is necessary for you to be born again.' Nicodemus had to be born again because it was the only way he could enter into the blessings which he apparently sought in coming to Christ that night.

Our Lord's words were primarily intended to penetrate the veil of misunderstanding which lay over the mind of Nicodemus. He was 'Israel's teacher' (Jn. 3:10), perhaps the most able theologian of his day and yet he could not take in the 'earthly things' which Jesus taught. How much less would he grasp heavenly things? (Jn. 3:12). Yes, '*you*, Nicodemus, need to be born again'. But what applied to Nicodemus applies to all. Unless *any man* is born again, he cannot see the kingdom of God. Unless *any man* is born again, he cannot enter the kingdom of God (Jn. 3:3, 5). *The necessity applies to all men, not only to Nicodemus.*

Why? Jesus supplies basically three answers.

(i) Man is flesh

'Flesh gives birth to flesh, but the Spirit gives birth to spirit' (Jn. 3:6), may simply mean that human nature is powerless to produce spiritual life and reality, as John's earlier use in John 1:13 would seem to indicate. This is not quite the same as Paul's use of 'flesh' to signify man in his sinfulness. But it would be impossible for John to think of man without recalling what he has become through his sin and rebellion against God. For him, as for Paul, it is axiomatic that 'flesh and blood cannot inherit the kingdom of God' (1 Cor. 15:50). Only a work of the Spirit can bring us into the kingdom of the Spirit.

(ii) Man cannot see

He is blind in his spirit, and 'cannot see the kingdom of God' (Jn. 3:3). 'See' in this context must mean to recognise, appreciate, or understand the significance of the kingdom. In Christ's own time this blindness was illustrated by the response men made to his great parables of the kingdom of God. Many who physically heard did not 'hear' the voice of Christ as he called them into his kingdom. They saw in their minds the vivid pictures which he portrayed but did not 'see' the figure of the

Saviour himself striding through the parables to engage them in Christian discipleship (Matt. 13:13–15).

This blindness was also characteristic of Nicodemus. Sadly it is sometimes characteristic of men and women who have given themselves to the religious life. In all their *doing* there is little *seeing*. I remember that being brought home forcefully to me as a student attending a conference at which the speaker was a well-known churchman of his time. When one of my friends fell into conversation with his wife, in the most natural way possible she confessed that she did not know what being 'born again' meant. (Of course, in their zeal, young men may speak about these things in crude and ill-informed terms and be off-putting in the extreme. But the very reverse was the case in this instance, and my friend was the most tactful and maturely sensitive of people!) The confession of the lady was but the simple and honest truth. So, in a similar open-hearted confession, Nicodemus asked Jesus: 'How can this be,' (Jn. 3:9). He could not see the kingdom, nor was he yet so convicted of his own need that he saw the necessity of a heavenly birth if he were ever to enter it.

But men are not only *blind*. They are shrouded in darkness. Later in the same chapter it is emphasised that men are in the dark, love the darkness, and hide from the light. They *are* darkness, says Paul (Eph. 5:8) and do the deeds of darkness (Eph. 5:11). They belong to the kingdom of darkness and are under its sway (Col. 1:13). But it is the glory of the gospel that God shines his light into the darkness, and it is the function of divine calling to summon us out of it (1 Pet. 2:9). But as yet Nicodemus had only the haziest idea of this. *Indeed he seems to have shared with his fellow-Pharisees and their many successors the delusion that instead of being a blind man in the dark, he was a sighted man in the light!* He sits in darkness before the Light of the world and as yet no hint of recognition crosses his face. He comes under our Lord's later warning: 'For judgment I have come into this world, so that the blind will see and those who see will become blind' (Jn. 9:39). The greatest tragedy is to think that the darkness in which we sit is in fact light, and that the light of Christ is really a dark shadow from which we should turn! Yet nothing is more characteristic of men's idea of the kingdom of God and of God himself.

No one has captured this spirit better than C. S. Lewis in his final Narnia tale, *The Last Battle*. Towards the End of Time he pictures a group of dwarfs met by the children who have entered the mysterious kingdom of Narnia. Aslan, Narnia's Saviour and Lion-King appears. The scene which follows illustrates the profound difference between the members of Christ's kingdom, and what they see, and those who stay outside it:

> 'Aslan,' said Lucy through her tears, 'could you—will you—do something for these poor Dwarfs?'
> 'Dearest,' said Aslan, 'I will show you both what I can, and what I cannot, do.' He came close to the Dwarfs and gave a low growl: low, but it set all the air shaking. But the Dwarfs said to one another, 'Hear that? That's the gang at the other end of the Stable. Trying to frighten us. They do it with a machine of some kind. Don't take any notice. They won't take *us* in again.'
> Aslan raised his head and shook his mane. Instantly a glorious feast appeared on the Dwarf's knees: pies and tongues and pigeons and trifles and ices, and each Dwarf had a goblet of good wine in his right hand. But it wasn't much use. They began eating and drinking greedily enough, but it was clear that they couldn't taste it properly. They thought they were eating and drinking only the sort of things you might find in a Stable. One said he was trying to eat hay and another said he had got a bit of an old turnip and a third said he'd found a raw cabbage leaf. And they raised golden goblets of rich red wine to their lips and said 'Ugh! Fancy drinking dirty water out of a trough that a donkey's been at! Never thought we'd come to this.' But very soon every Dwarf began suspecting that every other Dwarf had found something nicer than he had, and they started grabbing and snatching, and went on to quarrelling, till in a few minutes there was a free fight and all the good food was smeared on their faces and clothes or trodden under foot. But when at last they sat down to nurse their black eyes and their bleeding noses, they all said:
> 'Well, at any rate there's no Humbug here. We haven't let anyone take us in. The Dwarfs are for the Dwarfs.'
> 'You see,' said Aslan. 'They will not let us help them.

They have chosen cunning instead of belief. Their prison is only in their own minds, yet they are in that prison; and so afraid of being taken in that they cannot be taken out.'
C. S. Lewis, *The Last Battle*, pp. 134–5

Truly, like the Dwarfs, 'men loved darkness instead of light . . . and will not come into the light for fear . . .' (Jn. 3:19–20).

(iii) Man is powerless

He *cannot* enter the kingdom of God. Without the divine birth, Jesus says that man is weak (cf. Rom. 5:6). If he is to have the ability to see spiritually and to enter the kingdom by faith, it is essential that God should work in his life to enable him to do so. In fact this is common biblical teaching. The natural man does not and cannot receive spiritual reality (1 Cor. 2:14). The carnal mind is at enmity with God, and neither wills, nor is able to do, God's will (Rom. 7:7–8).

We rarely take this teaching sufficiently seriously, perhaps because it cuts from under our feet the last vestiges of our natural self-sufficiency. It highlights the biblical teaching that our salvation is all of grace. *The one thing necessary is the one thing we ourselves cannot perform!* It is this which gives point to our singing:

> *Nothing in my hand I bring,*
> *Simply to thy Cross I cling;*
> *Naked, come to thee for dress;*
> *Helpless, look to thee for grace;*
> *Foul, I to the fountain fly;*
> *Wash me, Saviour, or I die.*
> Augustus Montague Toplady

Only God can bring us to spiritual rebirth:
> *Thou must save, and Thou alone.*

The Character of Regeneration

Heavenly birth

The new birth is, *firstly*, heavenly in origin. Over and over again Christ emphasised this to Nicodemus. He needed to be born of water 'and the Spirit', for only the Spirit gives birth to spirit. Just as the wind blows wherever it pleases, 'So it is with everyone born of the Spirit.' Indeed the principle is heavily underlined by the expression 'born again'. The word John uses, translated 'again', can mean either *again* or *from above*. It is difficult to be dogmatic about its significance here. On the one hand, Nicodemus appears to follow through Jesus' words in terms of being born 'again' i.e. for a second time. He raises the question whether someone can re-enter the womb. But the other uses of the word in John strengthen the case for translating 'from above'. In John 3:31; 19:11, 23, it conveys the idea *from the top downwards*. If we take it in this sense then we are still able to make sense of Nicodemus' response. When Jesus tells him that he needs to be born from above, only faintly understanding the meaning, he lamely asks whether another birth is possible.

The corollary of this is often ignored. If *we* are members of that kingdom it must be by heavenly birth! In other words, if we are Christians it can only be because God has wonderfully intervened to give us new life. Every Christian ought to think long and hard about this, because we have an inevitable and at times very worldly tendency to regard some 'conversions' as being more wonderful or amazing than others. 'Miraculous' we say when a famous celebrity is 'born again', and of course we are right. But the miracle involved in the new birth of John or James Smith, whose name never appears in either Christian or secular press, is no less miraculous, no less wonderful and no less a cause of joy in heaven. It involves the same exercise of divine power and the same abundance of God's love. What we need to do, therefore, if we would enter into the joys of our new birth is *not* to cast a glance over our shoulder enviously regarding the spiritual biography of another, but to search the Scriptures to see the rich measure of grace that God pours into every new child of God!

God-given life

Regeneration is, *secondly*, sovereignly bestowed. Our Lord means nothing less than this by his words: 'The wind blows wherever it pleases. You hear its sound, but you cannot tell where it comes from or where it is going. So it is with everyone born of the Spirit' (Jn. 3:8). It is not surprising that Nicodemus, schooled in the religion of *doing* rather than *receiving*, replied in total bewilderment: 'How can this be?' (Jn. 3:9). This is the perennial reaction of the mind which sees the way to God as the way of human effort and what the New Testament calls 'the works of the law' (Gal. 2:16; 3:2, 5, 10). But for the first disciples of Jesus, schooled in the way of God's free grace, the enjoyment of salvation begins with *something God does*. We have already seen this in John; it is taught also by Peter; 'Praise be to the God and Father of our Lord Jesus Christ.' In his great mercy *he has given us new birth* into a living hope through the word of truth, 'that we might be a kind of first-fruits of all he created' (Jas. 1:18). We find the same in Paul: '*God raised us up with Christ* . . . For it is by grace you have been saved, through faith—and this not from yourselves, it is the gift of God . . . For *we are God's workmanship*, created in Christ Jesus to do good works, which God prepared in advance for us to do' (Eph. 2:6–10).

It may be objected that to place so much initiative in the hands of God is to remove all responsibility from the shoulders of man. But this is to misunderstand. To say that regeneration takes place by divine initiative does not deny that men must repent and believe in Christ. Jesus taught that regeneration is a sovereign, divine act. But when one enquirer raised mental objections to such evangelical doctrine by asking: 'Lord, are only a few people going to be saved?', Jesus' reply was: 'Make every effort to enter through the narrow door' (Lk. 13:24). In a word: Do not confuse things that differ. *Your duty is to make sure you have followed in the way of salvation yourself.*

Transforming power

In the *third* place, the New Testament indicates that the transforming power of regeneration is total. It meets our needs at every point. This is not to say that regeneration produces perfection. But just as total depravity means sin has influenced every area of our lives, so grace reaches into every aspect of our experience where the ravages of sin first ventured. It is through the new birth that the image of God, like an embryo in the womb, is restored. It then begins to grow to that full maturity of the later stages of Christian experience. In the conversation with Nicodemus several areas of this transformation appear to be hinted at in Jesus' words.

In regeneration *the mind is illuminated*. We see the kingdom of God. Is it not one of the greatest privileges of a living Christian fellowship, to witness a new Christian confessing, 'Once I was blind, but now I see'? To become a child of God by regeneration is to be given a totally new perspective on oneself and on others (how frequently young people will admit that only when they became children of God did they begin to see the needs of their parents and want to love and care for them). We see the world with new eyes: *Something lives in every hue that Christless eyes have never seen*, we now sing!

In regeneration *the heart is purified*. This is at least part of the meaning of the enigmatic words of Christ about being 'born of water' (Jn. 3:5). Many interpretations have been forwarded for this expression. Probably Jesus is referring to water as a symbol of purification. Undoubtedly that would be the major association to the mind of a Pharisee, and perhaps the recent events at Jordan would add point to his words. (Nicodemus had probably been to hear John the Baptist preach on the necessity of a baptism of repentance for the washing away of sins.) This, after all, was the promise God gave through Ezekiel about the New Covenant! 'I will sprinkle clean water on you, and you will be clean; I will cleanse you from all your impurities . . .' (Ezek. 36:25). Nicodemus, the Teacher of Israel could not fail to recall the words.

But what is a purified heart? What does Paul mean when he says to the Corinthians, 'You were washed . . .' (1 Cor. 6:11)? He means that in the work of giving us new spiritual life God creates in us new tendencies and dispositions towards right living. He puts his law in our hearts, so that the motivation to glorify and serve him in the paths of righteousness is no longer an external force but an inward power.

In regeneration *the desires are renewed*. What is born of flesh is flesh, but that to which the Spirit gives birth is spirit and has the characteristics of the Spirit. This seed thought is worked out more fully by Paul in Romans 8:5–8. The mind of the flesh is hostile to God and does not submit to his law. It cannot please God and walks on the road to death. All its desires are turned from God to self-pleasing. It has no taste for spiritual realities but turns from them and may even despise them like the Dwarfs in Lewis's Narnia. But the newly-born child of God craves for pure spiritual milk so that by it he may grow. He has tasted that the Lord is good and he wants more! (1 Pet. 2:2–3). Regeneration creates new desires to worship God, know his truth, meet his people, serve his kingdom and love and honour his Son. These aspirations are not perfect. They ebb and flow. At times we lament their weakness. But however far short we confess ourselves to have fallen from what we ought to be, we are not what we once were. Our minds are now set on the things above, where Christ is (Col. 3:1–2).

In regeneration *we begin to live a new life*. This is a major emphasis in 1 John where the doctrine of regeneration is dealt with more fully. Everyone who lives righteously is born of God (1 Jn. 2:29). This righteous living expresses itself in three ways: the one who is born of God loves his fellow-believers (1 Jn. 4:7), he overcomes the world (1 Jn. 5:4), and he does not go on sinning (1 Jn. 3:9). The world around him is a chief source of temptation to sin (1 Jn. 2:15–17) but his relationship to it is radically altered. When it spreads out its enticing tentacles towards him he recognises that his new birth has made him a new creation in which those allurements will no longer conquer him. Similarly his attitude to his fellow-Christians becomes a thing of beauty—he loves them with an affection which is unparalleled. There is no more powerful testimony to the reality of a new birth than that bonding of human lives together in Christian fellowship which transcends the barriers of ordinary relationships. But can we agree with John that to be born again is no longer to go on sinning? We will have to return to this question in chapter 13. But here it is important for us not to play John's words off against our own experience and water down his teaching. If Christ came to be our Saviour; if one of the focal points of that salvation is in the deliverance of his people from the bondage of sin, then there must be some sense in which John's words can be taken at their face value. The new birth radically and totally transforms our relationship to sin. Christ Jesus makes men whole, and has begun the process of making all things new! This is what it means to be 'born again' from above.

Lord, I was blind! I could not see
In thy marred visage any grace;
But now the beauty of thy face
In radiant vision dawns on me.

> *Lord, I was deaf! I could not hear*
> * The thrilling music of thy voice;*
> * But now I hear thee and rejoice,*
> *And all thine uttered words are dear.*
>
> *Lord, I was dumb! I could not speak*
> * The grace and glory of thy Name;*
> * But now, as touched with living flame,*
> *My lips thine eager praises wake.*
>
> *Lord, I was dead! I could not stir*
> * My lifeless soul to come to thee;*
> * But now, since thou hast quickened me,*
> *I rise from sin's dark sepulchre.*
>
> *Lord, thou hast made the blind to see,*
> * The deaf to hear, the dumb to speak,*
> * The dead to live; and lo, I break*
> *The chains of my captivity!*
>   William Tidd Matson

Praise be to the God and Father of our Lord Jesus Christ! In his great mercy he has given us new birth into a living hope! (1 Pet. 1:3).

The connecting link between our new birth and our living hope is *Faith*.

7
Faith in Christ

Regeneration, the implanting of a new life within us, is inseparable from the repentance and faith by which we enter the kingdom of God. When a man is born again he sees and enters the kingdom of God (Jn. 3:3, 5), and he does so invariably by repentance towards God and faith in Jesus Christ.

We may tend to think, largely on the basis of the order in which the words appear, that Scripture teaches that repentance precedes faith in our experience. On occasion that position is outlined something like this: we will never come to trust in Christ until we feel sorry for our sins, so repentance must always be first. That is mistaken and unhelpful thinking—mistaken, because it confuses repentance with conviction of sin; and unhelpful, because it tends to promote the view that a fixed degree of 'repentance' is necessary as a kind of qualification for faith. But this is evidently not the position of the New Testament. Conviction is not repentance. And in any case the deepest levels of conviction may be experienced *after* rather than *before* conversion.

In fact there is a sense in which we must think of the relationship between repentance and faith the other way round. Repentance can only be truly evangelical when it is based on faith in God and in his word. This is the position of the writer of Psalm 130: 'But with you there is forgiveness; *therefore* you are feared' (Ps. 130:4). It was because he saw and trusted the forgiving grace of God that he feared him in his repentance. Similarly on the Day of Pentecost Peter counsels his hearers, 'Repent and be baptised, every one of you, in the name of Jesus Christ so that your sins may be forgiven' (Acts 2:38). The summons holds out the word of forgiveness to them in the expectation that, grasping the promise by faith, they will be drawn in to Christ by the rope of repentance! So faith and repentance must be seen as marriage partners and never separated.

'Faith' in Scripture

It may come as a surprise to learn that even in the A.V. translation of the Old Testament the word 'faith' is used only twice! In both of these instances it has been suggested the translation is inaccurate! In Deuteronomy 32:20 it should have been rendered 'faithfulness', and some scholars argue for the same translation in Habbakuk 2:4. But statistics are not normally an adequate base for biblical doctrine. It is clear from the rest of the Old Testament, and from the New Testament's comments, that faith played a central role in the lives of men of God under the Old Covenant. Hebrews 11, for example, catalogues many of the great heroes of the old dispensation and emphasises the quality of their faith as an example for us. Furthermore the gospel to which the Law and the Prophets bear witness (Rom. 3:21) can be preached from an Old Testament text. In Romans Paul draws out his whole doctrine of justification by faith from Habakkuk 2:4. So, however infrequently the expression 'faith' is used, the *fact* of faith is a great reality in the Old as well as the New Testament.

In fact in the Old Testament faith is often expressed by the ideas of 'trust and obey'. It is related to the idea of leaning on, entrusting oneself to, or having confidence in something. So in many places, particularly in the Psalms, we find expressions of this saving trust (Ps. 4:5; 9:10; 22:4; 25:2 etc.). It is trust in God's character and obedience to his living voice expressed in his word. Consequently the *object of faith* in the Old Testament is *the promise of God* which awaits its fulfilment in the coming of Christ. Faith looked forward then, just as now it looks backward to its object in Christ. It is interesting to notice how this is expressed in the teaching of Hebrews that 'faith is being sure of *what we hope for* and certain of what we do not see' (Heb. 11:1). In fact this prospective characteristic runs through the whole of Hebrews 11—Noah trusted God's word about 'things not seen' (v. 7), and along with Abel, Enoch and Abraham 'did not receive the things promised; they only saw them and welcomed them from a distance' (v. 13). The writer of the letter pays them this glowing tribute: 'All these people were still living by faith when they died.' Even the martyrs who were commended for their faith did not receive what had been promised (v. 39). Faith for them was hearing the testimony of God, trusting his promise, and living in the light of God's faithfulness to it.

In the New Testament the words for 'faith' and 'belief' each occur about two hundred and forty times, appearing in every book with the exception of 2 and 3 John.

What is Faith?

Faith is a great biblical word, but its currency has been taken over, unfortunately, by religious language in general. As we have seen, in Scripture faith is generally the living personal trust in Christ. But it is common to hear other religions today described as 'other faiths' even although faith in the biblical sense may have no part to play in them. Biblical faith is a much richer and fuller notion altogether, and consists of several elements.

(i) Knowledge

Faith is dependent on what can be known about God. Even more significantly, in the New Testament faith involves us in coming to a knowledge of God himself. This is the great joy which Christ shared with his Father in the High Priestly Prayer of John 17: 'This is eternal life: that they may know you, the only true God, and Jesus Christ, whom you have sent' (Jn. 17:3). Our Lord's words are to be understood in the light of John 1:18, 'No-one has ever seen God, but God the only (Son), who is at the Father's side, *has made him known.*' The word which is used in the original is the root from which we get the word 'exegesis', the explanation and exposition of Scripture. What John is saying is that Jesus is the 'exegesis' of God, and makes him known clearly to us. It is the same teaching we find in Matthew 11:27, 'No-one knows the Son except the Father, and no-one knows the Father except the Son and those to whom the Son chooses to reveal him.' The revelation of the Father by the Son to the disciples, through faith, brings them to the knowledge of God.

All trust is ultimately dependent on knowledge. The problem we have in allowing complete strangers to take possession of our belongings is just that we do not know them well enough to trust them! But the knowledge involved in faith is not merely intellectual baggage, because true knowledge in the Bible invariably involves personal fellowship. The deep personal relationship of a man with his wife is described in these terms. This kind of knowledge does not mean that we analyse its object from a distance, scrutinising it objectively and dispassionately. It is the kind of knowledge that brings us into immediate contact with God himself. There is no greater privilege open to man than knowing God and this is what is held out to us through faith.

(ii) Assent

While it is important to see intimate fellowship with God as its primary aspect, faith also involves recognising certain things as true and giving mental assent to them. Believing in Christ means assenting to the truth about Christ as well as coming to know him. In fact there is a sense in which we may come to believe against our wishes! It was so with Saul of Tarsus and has been with multitudes since that they have come to faith despite their unwillingness, because the evidence which has persuaded them has proved to be so overpoweringly strong. We speak in ordinary life about a man being so trustworthy that we would be compelled to trust him against our will. So B. B. Warfield wrote: 'The conception embodied in the terms "belief", "faith", in other words, is not that of an arbitrary act of the subject's; it is that of a mental state or act which is determined by sufficient reasons.' (*Biblical and Theological Studies*, p. 376), and John Murray adds to Warfield's suggestion:

> Faith is *forced* consent. That is to say, when evidence is judged by the mind to be sufficient, the state of mind we call 'faith' is the inevitable precipitate. It is not something we can resist or in respect of which we suspend judgment. In such a case faith is compelled, it is demanded, it is commanded. For whenever the reasons are apprehended or judged sufficient, will we, nill we, faith or belief is induced. Will to the contrary, desire to the contrary, overwhelming interest to the contrary, cannot make us believe the opposite of our judgment with respect to the evidence.
>
> For example we say a man commands confidence. We do not trust a man simply because we have willed to, or even because we desire to. And we cannot distrust a man simply

because we wish or will to do so. We trust a man because we have evidence that to us appears sufficient, evidence of trustworthiness. When to our apprehension a man presents evidence of trustworthiness we cannot but trust him, even though we hate his trustworthiness and would wish the opposite to be the case ... (e.g. the criminal who wants to evade justice, arraigned before a judge whom he believes to be just and fair, may do everything in his power to do away with the judge. But why? Because he trusts him).
Collected Writings II. p. 237

Naturally, if faith were merely assent this would imply a very different picture from the biblical one. Faith is more than assent, but it is never *less* than assent. Thomas' faith in the risen Christ was assent to the fact of the resurrection. But it was more. It was a heart which acknowledged, 'My Lord and my God!' (Jn. 20:28).

(iii) Trust in Christ

This is the heart of faith. Although 'trusting in Christ' is not a predominant expression in the New Testament, these words certainly focus attention on a central feature in the biblical teaching. It was because this element was lacking in the 'faith' of those who believed in Jesus only because of his mighty works, that he declined to entrust himself to them (Jn. 2:23–5). This summons to trust Christ constantly appears in his invitations to follow him, and especially in his 'gracious words', 'Come to me, all you who are weary and burdened, and I will give you rest. Take my yoke upon you and learn from me, for I am gentle and humble in heart, and you will find rest for your souls' (Matt. 11:28–9). Other biblical ideas which are synonymous with faith further underscore this principle of personal trust. Faith means abiding in Christ (Jn. 15:1–11); it means receiving Christ (Jn. 1:12) and therefore embracing him in total trust.

Such trust is always a costly thing, because it involves us in surrendering our lives to Christ. That is why in the Synoptic Gospels (Matthew, Mark and Luke) Jesus does not speak simply of 'faith'. He speaks about *following* and about *carrying the cross*. He does this to emphasise what faith involves. It means the practical recognition that Jesus is the Lord of our lives. It means forsaking everything for his sake. It means sacrifice and service.

This is why the New Testament illustrates the nature of faith by the life of Moses (Heb. 11:23-28). For him it involved the renunciation of worldly honour and wealth. It meant commitment to a people who would suffer constant reproach, and the acceptance of ill-treatment with them instead of experiencing the pleasures of sin. What possible motivation makes such a man abandon himself to the life of faith? It was the value of having Christ! 'He regarded disgrace for the sake of Christ as of greater value than the treasures of Egypt' (Heb. 11:26). This is the sure mark of the man of faith: he clings to Christ alone as Saviour, and he commits himself to Christ alone as his Lord.

VARIETY IN FAITH

While these are essential characteristics of faith, we must not forget that it has other dimensions. True faith takes its character and quality from its object and not from itself. Faith gets a man out of himself and into Christ. Its strength therefore depends on the character of Christ. Even those of us who have weak faith have the same strong Christ as others!

(i) Degrees of faith

Faith is liable to greater and less degrees. The New Testament speaks of *little faith* (Matt. 6:30; 8:26, 14:31; 16:8) and *great faith* (Matt. 8:10; 15:28); of *weak faith* and *strong faith* (Rom. 4:19-20); of *growing faith* (2 Thess. 1:3), *unfeigned or sincere faith* (2 Tim. 1:5), *sound faith* (Tit. 1:13; 2:2), men who are *full of faith* (Acts 6:5, 8; 11:24) and those who enjoy the *full assurance of faith* (Heb. 10:22); of *all faith* (1 Cor. 13:2) and of *shipwrecked faith* (1 Tim. 1:19). The object of faith does not change—Christ is the same yesterday, today and for ever. But our love for him, our knowledge of his goodness, our acquaintance with his ways, our experience of his power may grow and in proportion to that growth comes a strengthening of faith. Strong faith in Christ draws on the resources of his grace and sets us free from many of the inhibitions that bind our lives. Strong faith enables us to use to the full the gifts God has given to us (Rom. 12:3). At the same time Paul teaches us the importance of recognising the measure of faith we have and not despising others or criticising them because their faith is either weaker or stronger than our own (Rom. 14:1 ff). In the household of faith there is always change, development, progress and sometimes illness. The presence of faith among the people of God does not produce carbon-copy Christians. The church is always kept in the place where it is dependent upon the living Christ!

(ii) Kinds of faith

There are hints in the New Testament that there may also be different *kinds* of faith as well as different *degrees* of it. The faith of those who believed in Jesus because of his miracles (Jn. 2:23) does not seem to be the same kind of thing as saving faith. Certainly it produced a different response from Jesus. Similarly at the end of the Sermon on the Mount we find the warning of Jesus to those who claimed to have performed miracles in his name, 'Then I will tell them plainly, "I never knew you. Away from me, you evildoers!" ' (Matt. 7:23). Is this what Paul was to call the faith which could remove mountains but lacked love (1 Cor. 13:2)? Apparently the faith by which spiritual gifts are exercised is not necessarily saving faith. The New Testament is adamant that gifts are not grace and may even be exercised apart from the experience of grace. This is a warning to all who have received a gift of the Spirit, whether of preaching, ruling, or pastoring, or of any other kind.

But true faith, saving, trusting faith, which is our *response to* the grace of God, is also *a gift* of the grace of God. However we interpret Ephesians 2:8, 'For it is by grace you have been saved, through faith—and this not from yourselves, it is the gift of God' (which certainly seems to indicate that faith is something which God gives), Paul later indicates in the same letter that faith is 'from God the Father and the Lord Jesus Christ' (Eph. 6:23). Not that God believes for us; that would lead us to the crassest form of fatalism. *We* believe in Christ, and God does not and cannot believe for us. But the faith with which we believe and trust is only ours because he has created it within our hearts. When we find ourselves saying: 'Lord, I believe, help my unbelief', then we have reached another landmark in the outworking of God's plan of salvation.

8
True Repentance

We have already noted that faith and repentance are twin doctrines and cannot be separated. All true evangelical experience necessarily involves both. If we truly believe in Christ it must be penitently; if we repent of sin it must be believingly. Furthermore, these twin responses to the grace of God are not only joined together at their birth, they remain inseparable throughout the whole of life. Just as we continue to trust in Christ as our Saviour and Lord, we continue in the life of repentance. It is in this sense that John Calvin understands repentance when he defines it in these terms:

> repentance . . . is the true turning of our life to God, a turning that arises from a pure and earnest fear of him; and it consists in the mortification of our flesh and of the old man, and in the vivification of the Spirit.
> *Institutes*, III. iii. 5

Although we are still at the stage of considering the privileges and experiences which stand at the gate to the Christian life, we must not lose sight of this life-long dimension in repentance.

THE NATURE OF REPENTANCE

In the *Old Testament* several ideas are included in the vocabulary for repentance. The word *nacham* expresses a sense of sorrow sometimes including the consequence of a change of purpose or action. In another form it refers more to the consequences of sorrow, and conveys the idea of comforting oneself. It may be that included the general idea that through repentance one discovers a psychological release and comfort. These words can even be used of God in the Old Testament. The most important word theologically is *shub* which means 'to return'. It conveys the idea of leaving something behind, being quit with it. It has strong physical connotations and is used of the people's return from exile in Babylon to Jerusalem where God had promised the blessing of his presence with them. This is the heart of repentance. It is a returning to God.

Generally the idea of repentance in the Old Testament is associated with external evidences of its presence (see 1 Kings 21:27; Isaiah 58:5; Nehemiah 9:1; Hosea 7:14; Jonah 3:8). Sometimes in Old Testament religion these expressions of repentance were corrupted into means of penance, as though God could be impressed by mere externals, and as though repentance were a meritorious work. But at no time did the Old Testament countenance this—it is a book without a trace of legalism. At other times the view of repentance adopted was both superficial and mechanistic. This seems to have been the case in the days of Hosea, and he pin-points it in words which have come to form the basis of one of the most beautiful and poignant of all scripture paraphrases:

> Come let us return to the Lord. He has torn us to pieces but he will heal us; he has injured us but he will bind up our wounds.
>
> After two days he will revive us; on the third day he will restore us, that we may live in his presence.
>
> Hosea 6:1-2

To which the divine word of response is:

> What can I do with you, Ephraim?
> What can I do with you, Judah?
> Your love is like the morning mist,
> like the early dew that disappears.
>
> Hosea 6:4

In contrast with their bland assumptions of God's favour, the prophet recognises that repentance is always a much more costly thing than Israel knew. So Isaiah points the people to the true repentance for which God looks, which is ethical in its fruit and leads to new life. 'Rend *your heart* and not *your garments*' is Joel's cry (Joel 2:13). True repentance is inward, not merely external or superficial.

Under the ministry of the prophets the people were called to a true repentance to return in a spiritual and moral sense to God. This call to repentance focused attention on the covenant which God had made with them (as, for example, Hosea 6:7 indicates). They were a people who stood in breach of God's provision for them. To the covenant, and to God in the covenant they must return.

In the Old Testament three things provided evidence that genuine repentance had taken place. (i) a new *trust* in the Lord—'in quietness and trust is your strength,' said Isaiah (30:15). (ii) Of this the first-fruits would be *obedience*, a measure of which had formerly been seen in Jeremiah's day, 'Recently you repented and did what is right in my sight: Each of you proclaimed freedom to his countrymen. You even made a covenant before me in the house that bears my name' (Jer. 34:15). (iii) That obedience was specifically manifested in *a rejection of ungodliness* and a return to the ways of the covenant. Man should turn from his wicked ways (Jer. 26:3; 36:3). This was a truth for the whole nation to hear, but it was also something for each individual, as Ezekiel made so powerfully plain (Ezek. 3:19; 18:21, 23, 27; 33:12, 14, 19). If a man turns from his wicked ways, he will discover that repentance leads to life (Ezek. 18:21-3). It is very interesting to notice the basis on which Ezekiel makes these appeals: 'Get a new heart and a new spirit. Why will you die, O house of Israel?' (Ezek. 18:31). It is not only in the teaching of Jesus that the great prerequisite to faith and repentance is the new birth!

In some English versions of the *New Testament* two words are translated by 'repent': *metanoeō*, to change one's mind and *metamelomai* which really means to regret rather than to repent.

True repentance (*metanoia*) is the return to God with which the Christian life begins, continues and ends. Repentance is the Prodigal Son making his way from the far country to the Father, to serve him and receive his embrace. That return was certainly prompted by a sense of regret, 'How many of my father's hired men have food to spare, and here I am starving to death' (Lk. 15:17). Repentance here, however, means more than regret. It means a change of direction.

The apostle Paul uses both words in the same context in 2 Corinthians 7, and this clarifies the distinction. He speaks there of a repentance which is not regretted (2 Cor. 7:10) which is the product of sorrow. But, he adds, it is possible to feel sorrow without ever repenting towards God.

Elements in Repentance

The *Westminster Shorter Catechism* asks the question: *What is repentance unto life?* and answers:

> Repentance unto life is a saving grace, whereby a sinner out of a true sense of his sin, and apprehension of the mercy of God in Christ, doth with grief and hatred of his sin, turn from it unto God, with full purpose of, and endeavour after, new obedience.

What is involved in repentance? The experience and depth of emotion in repentance will differ from person to person and will depend on a very large variety of circumstances in their lives. But certain characteristics are commonly present in all repentance.

(i) A *sense of shame*. We come to see that our sin has degraded us, and more important, despoiled God of the image of his glory in us. The beginnings of repentance are often accompanied by a sense of this personal dis-grace of God and ourselves. So Paul speaks to the Romans of the things which *now* make them ashamed (Rom. 6:21).

(ii) This leads to *humbling*. In a strange way a man who begins to feel shame at some past misdeed may discover a spirit of pride welling up within himself. He may begin to defend and justify himself and thus harden his heart. But when God works true repentance, our mouths are shut, we confess our guilt before God and are humbled before his throne (Rom. 3:19).

(iii) Thus humbled, *sorrow and regret* fill our hearts. It is both natural and necessary that we should long that what has been might not have been; that we should grieve and mourn over the despite we have done to God, to others and to ourselves. How we regret the wasted privileges and the wasted years!

(iv) But this is not yet repentance. For these characteristics but pave the way to produce *a distaste of sin for what it is*. This is part of conviction, that we taste the real nature of our sin. It is part of divine illumination, that we see it in all its ugly horror. We do not merely regret is inconveniences and its consequences in our own experience, but we find ourselves crying out with David:

> I know my transgressions,
> and my sin is always before me.
> Against you, you only have I sinned
> and done what is evil in your sight, ...
>
> Surely I have been a sinner from my birth,
> sinful from the time my mother conceived me.
> Psalm 51:3–5

And we say with William Cowper:

> *I hate the sin that made thee mourn*
> *And drove thee from my breast*

(v) But there is another element which is all too often and easily forgotten, perhaps because it scarcely seems consistent with these other aspects. True repentance always involves *the recognition of the pardon of God*. As the Westminster Shorter Catechism rightly saw, we repent because we have an 'apprehension of the mercy of God in Christ'. It is the grace of God which teaches us to fear as well as relieves our fears!

The classic illustration of this is found in Psalm 130, which Martin Luther called 'a Pauline Psalm' for this very reason. There the Psalmist is conscious of his sin to the point of being quite overwhelmed: he cries to God out of the depths (v. 1). He knows that if God kept a record of his sins, he could not hope to stand (v. 3). Yet his hope is this: 'with you there is forgiveness; therefore you are feared ... with the Lord is unfailing love and with him is full redemption' (Ps. 130:4, 7). Only when we turn away from looking at our own sin to look at the face of God, to find his pardoning grace, do we begin to repent. Only by seeing that there is grace and forgiveness with him would we ever dare to repent and thus return to the fellowship and presence of the Father.

This is why in the New Testament repentance is seen as a gift of the gospel which comes to us through Christ (Acts 5:31; 11:18, cf. 2 Tim. 2:25). It is, says Paul, the kindness of God which leads us to repentance (Rom. 2:4). The law may lead to conviction, exposing a sense of guilt and need, as it did also in Paul's experience (Rom. 7:7-13). But only when grace appears on the horizon offering forgiveness will the sunshine of the love of God melt our hearts and draw us back to him.

SIGNS OF REPENTANCE

From the beginning of the biblical teaching on repentance it is clear that it has certain moral characteristics. It is never merely a sense of regret at wrong-doing, or a deeply felt conviction of guilt. It is a return to God and to a life marked by the light of God in our lives. Writing to the Ephesians Paul indicates this:

> For you were once darkness, but now you are light in the Lord. Live as children of light (for the fruit of the light consists in all goodness, righteousness and truth) and find out what pleases the Lord.
>
> Ephesians 5:8-10

The classic passage on the evidences of repentance however is 2 Corinthians 7:8-11.

> I see that my letter hurt you, but only for a little while—yet now I am happy, not because you were made sorry, but because your sorrow led you to repentance. For you became sorrowful as God intended and so were not harmed in any way by us. Godly sorrow brings repentance that leads to salvation and leaves no regret, but worldly sorrow brings death. See what this godly sorrow has produced in you: what earnestness, what eagerness to clear yourselves, what indignation, what alarm, what longing, what concern, what readiness to see justice done.

These words refer of course to an abnormal instance of repentance, and they also clearly refer to a corporate experience. But nevertheless the evidences of the Corinthians' repentance illustrate the marks which will appear in all true repentance. Paul mentions seven things.

(i) *Earnestness*. The word (*spoudē*) suggests that the Corinthians had now adopted a serious and right attitude to their situation, one which was consistent with its gravity. *Before*, they had shown carelessness and indifference to their manner of life. *Now* they were transformed into men and women conscious of the way in which God viewed their sin. So the penitent is always a man who has begun to see his life and his sin from the divine perspective. There is nothing more calculated to bring sobriety to the heart which has been intoxicated with a spirit of indifference towards God.

(ii) *Eagerness to clear themselves*. The expression (*apologia*) means a defence of oneself against charges. That might suggest the idea of self-defence which is far removed from genuine repentance, but in all likelihood Paul here means that the *apologia* took the form of rectifying their faults. Now that their guilt had become a matter of consequence to them, they were concerned to deal with the cause of it with the help of God.

(iii) *Indignation* probably suggests the idea of *vexation* with themselves, and a new attitude of hatred and opposition to what they had done. Elsewhere in the New Testament the verbal form of the same word is used in the sense of showing displeasure (e.g. Matt. 21:15; 26:8 etc.).

(iv) *Alarm* (*phobos*) means fear. It is not clear what the object of this fear was. It could have been Paul! After all, he had written to them in his first letter, 'Shall I come to you with a whip, or in love with a gentle spirit? What do you prefer?' (1 Cor. 4:21, cf. 2 Cor. 7:8). Perhaps the fear was God-directed, in which case it reflected their desire for forgiveness (Ps. 130:4). It may not be possible or necessary to decide. But whatever produced the fear it was the sign of a truly awakened conscience being brought under the disciplines of divine truth.

(v) *Longing* is not normally a characteristic we associate with repentance. But the context may provide us with the clue to Paul's thinking. What would create a sense of longing in their hearts but the alienation from God and his people (perhaps especially Paul) which their sin had caused? That is why in extreme cases excommunication may be necessary in the Christian church. It not only has restoration as its end, but is a means to that end, because it produces the circumstances which will make the excommunicant long to be restored to the privileges he formerly enjoyed.

(vi) *Concern* or *zeal* (A.V., R.S.V.). The word Paul uses is *zēlos*, jealousy. It signifies the exclusive focussing of our desires on a particular object. In this case that object may be Paul and his affection for them. Restoration to willing Christian service and participation in the ministry of men God has raised up as leaders is a genuine sign of repentance. In this passage one of the ways in which the repentance of the Corinthians is indicated is by their responsiveness to Paul's word to them—the sorrow his letter had produced led to repentance (vv. 8–9).

(vii) *Punishment* (R.S.V.) At the sight of this we naturally draw back! It is perhaps an unfortunate translation and the N.I.V. is certainly much more felicitous in its rendering 'readiness to see justice done'. The word means vengeance. It is the spirit of Zacchaeus who, recognising his past sin, wishes to make reparation and restoration for it wherever possible (Lk. 19:8). Repentance is thus not only a new way of life built on the promise of forgiveness, but one which reaches into the past in order that what can be repaired may be by God's grace.

This analysis of repentance impresses on us what a radical thing it always is. It affects our emotions, but its influence extends to every aspect of our being and challenges us in our relationships with others as well as with God. It is a mistake to think that we repent only once, at the beginning of the Christian life. Repentance means the whole of life returning to the purposes of God. Therefore it continues throughout our entire life.

But this continuing repentance will also have a beginning which is related to it as the seed is to the fruit. That seed is planted in us at regeneration when Christ's death to sin begins to find a grip upon our hearts. The paradox of spiritual growth is that as *faith* deepens and brings with it new levels of joy and assurance, so also *repentance* deepens bringing ever more profound an awareness of our need of Christ. The purpose of God is clear. The more we sense our need the more we shall find our need met in Christ. The more we find our need met in Christ the nearer we will come to him. The nearer we come to him the more we will discover our hearts saying: 'If you should mark my sins, Lord, I could not stand. But there is forgiveness with you that you may be feared.'

Wisely did Martin Luther, as he nailed his ninety-five Theses to the door of the Wittenberg church, choose as the first:

> Our Lord and Master Jesus Christ, in saying 'Repent ye' etc., intended that the whole of the life of believers should be repentance.

What, however, we should never lose sight of, is that the first springs of this repentance bring us into the privilege of being justified before a holy God. Both faith and repentance may grow and deepen. But the glory of justification, as the next chapter will unfold, is that it is perfect, complete and final from the beginning!

9
Justification

Martin Luther, whose grasp of the gospel was better than most, once said that the doctrine of Justification was the article by which the church stands or falls. 'This article', he said, 'is the head and cornerstone of the Church, which alone begets, nourishes, builds, preserves and protects the Church; without it the Church of God cannot subsist one hour.' Luther was right. Although for our understanding of the general shape and direction of the Christian life we have suggested the doctrine of regeneration is *important*, the doctrine of justification is *central*. Not only is it the article of the standing or falling church, but also of the standing or falling Christian. Probably more trouble is caused in the Christian life by an inadequate or mistaken view of this doctrine than any other. When the child of God loses his sense of peace with God, finds his concern for others dried up, or generally finds his sense of the sheer goodness and grace of God diminished, it is from this fountain that he has ceased to drink. Conversely, if we can gain a solid grounding here, we have the foundation for a life of peace and joy.

WHAT IS JUSTIFICATION?

In Scripture the words for justify and justification convey the idea of being righteous, or being in a right relationship. In contrast, in Greek moral philosophy righteousness was one of the four cardinal moral virtues (along with sobriety, goodness and piety) and fundamentally meant conformity to the accepted ethical norms of society in general. But in Scripture righteousness is of an altogether higher order. To be righteous in Scripture means to be rightly related to God and to his law.

Justification and righteousness are legal terms.

What is at stake in a court is the question—How is this person related to the law? In the United Kingdom that includes the question—How is this person related to the authority of the monarch? So a trial may be described as Regina (the Queen) v

do not have the sense of 'making righteous', but carry this declarative, constitutive sense (cf. Gen. 15:6; Ps. 32:1–2, and Paul's use of both texts in Rom. 4:3, 6–8).
(iv) The ultimate proof that justification involves a status changed by public declaration lies in the biblical view that through the resurrection Jesus himself was 'justified' (1 Tim. 3:16). It would be quite impossible to understand this in the sense of an alteration in our Lord's character. It must refer to the vindication of him by God through the triumph and victory of the resurrection. By the resurrection he was declared to be in a right relationship with God (cf. Rom. 1:4).

THE POWER OF JUSTIFICATION

The practical importance of this cannot be exaggerated. The glory of the gospel is that God has declared Christians to be rightly related to him in spite of their sin. But our greatest temptation and mistake is to try to smuggle character into his work of grace. How easily we fall into the trap of assuming that we only remain justified so long as there are grounds in our character for that justification. But Paul's teaching is that nothing we do ever contributes to our justification. So powerful was his emphasis on this that men accused him of teaching that it did not matter how they lived if God justified them. If God justifies us as we are, what is the point of holiness? There is still a sense in which this is a test of whether we offer the world the grace of God in the Gospel. Does it make men say: 'You are offering grace that is so free it doesn't make any difference how you live'? This was precisely the objection the Pharisees had to Jesus' teaching!

Justification is not subject to degrees. God's work *in us* is. We differ in the extent to which we allow his Spirit to make us like Christ, and it is possible therefore to be more or less Christ-like. But it is not possible to be more or less justified! Paul was not more justified than you are as a Christian! John Bunyan's long experience of conviction and a spirit of bondage did not make him a more justified man than you! Furthermore, there is no second verdict still awaited after justification; for justification is the verdict of the Last Assize of God brought forward into the present. The judgment we should receive then was brought for-is no-one righteous, not even one' (3:10), all will stand condemned (2:5–6). (iii) Further, says Paul in often misunderstood words, God's judgment will be according to the light which men have received (2:12–15). But this will inevitably lead to condemnation for those who have sinned without knowing the law, as well as those who have had the law revealed and broken its dictates. (iv) Finally, God will judge men according to Christ Jesus (2:16). In that light men are without excuse. To stand before God on the grounds of what we are or have achieved is to expose ourselves to the thoroughgoing condemnation of the God against whom we have sinned.

The only basis for justification which the New Testament recognises is *the work of Christ*. Of course the *source* of Christ's work, and therefore the source of our justification, resides in the love of God—*not for a moment should we countenance the caricature of biblical teaching, that a loving Saviour reconciles us to a grudging Father*. But love, as love alone, can never justify. The Judge in court cannot justify his guilty child in the dock on the grounds that he loves him. Something more must be done. The New Testament expresses the position thus: 'we are justified freely by his grace *through the redemption that came by Christ Jesus*. God presented him as a sacrifice of atonement through faith in his blood. He did this to demonstrate his justice . . .' (Rom. 3:24–5). The love of God is the source of our justification, but the death of Christ is its grounds. We 'have now been justified by his blood' (Rom. 5:9); the result of his obedient life and death is our justification (Rom. 5:18); just as he was delivered over to death for our sins he was raised because of our justification (Rom. 4:25).

All this is clear enough, but it leads us to ask: How and why can the work of Christ bring justification for the ungodly? How does it resolve the great issue of the early chapters of Romans? *How can God, being just in all his ways, justify the ungodly?* We can set out the answer in three basic stages. The first two indicate what Christ has done, the third indicates the relationship which Christ sustains to his people so that his accomplishments become theirs, and 'through the obedience of the one man (Christ) the many will be made righteous' (Rom. 5:19).

(i) *Christ lived a life of total obedience to God.* This is sometimes described as his 'active obedience'. He was 'born under law' (Gal. 4:4) and lived the whole of his life in the form of a servant of the law. Unlike all those whose nature he came to share by his incarnation, it was not necessary for Christ to receive the wages of sin in death. He was 'holy, blameless, pure, set apart from sinners' (Heb. 7:26), and therefore free from the penalties of a broken law.

(ii) *Christ, despite his personal innocence, was treated as a guilty man.* In one chapter of Luke's account of the passion of Jesus there are five confessions that Jesus was totally innocent (Lk. 23:4, 14, 22, 41, 47). Yet he was crucified as a criminal. The early church saw not only the hands of wicked men involved in this, but primarily the hand of God. The word which is used regularly about the Lord's death is that he was 'delivered up', or 'handed over' (e.g. Matt. 20:19; 26:15; 27:2, 18, 26 etc.). It is the same word Paul employs when he says—*God* did not spare his own Son, but *delivered him up* (Rom. 8:32). It is the same basic perspective on the Cross as the ancient insight of Isaiah, that it would please the Lord to bruise his Servant and put him to grief (Is. 53:10). This experience of suffering as though he were guilty of a breach of divine law is sometimes spoken of as Christ's 'passive obedience', not that he did not actively obey God through it all, but because his obedience took the form of a willing acceptance of the will of the Lord.

(iii) *The explanation of this mystery, that the sinless one suffered as the guilty one, is to be found in the bond which God has established between Christ and his people.* Christ became our brother-man through his incarnation so that he might represent us and substitute for us throughout his obedient life and especially in his death on the Cross. There he bore our sins and paid our debts. In several places in Scripture the idea which is stressed is that an *exchange* took place. Christ stood in my place and received the judgment which is really mine. Before God I stand as though I were in Christ's place so that I may receive Christ's judgment and be justified before God. The reality of this exchange is highlighted by the fact that the two crimes of which Jesus was accused were the crimes of which mankind was guilty in the Garden of Eden. By aspiring to be as God, and disobeying his royal law he committed *blasphemy* against the person of God and *treason* against his graciously constituted authority. Thus even the form of the charges brought against our Saviour indicates that he did not stand before the judgment seats of Caiaphas and Pilate to be condemned for his own crimes. In reality he stood before the Judgment Seat of God to receive the verdict of *guilty* as the Representative and Substitute for sinful men. So, in Christ a 'wonderful exchange' took place. He became what he was not, a condemned criminal, in order that we might become what we are not, men declared righteous and justified in the sight of God. This was so, as Paul points out in some of the most dramatic language in the New Testament, because he was made sin for us (although not himself a sinner) in order that we might become the righteousness of God in him. He came voluntarily under the curse of God, in order to set us at liberty from it (cf. 2 Cor. 5:21; Gal. 3:13). This is what justification really means.

Sometimes, however, we undervalue this grand teaching of Scripture and we do not feel its power the way we should. For example, it is sometimes said that 'justified' means *'just-if-I'd* never sinned'. Doubtless there is an element of truth in this but it does not do justice to the biblical teaching. For one thing it does not bring out sufficiently forcefully that it is the *ungodly* and the *guilty* who are justified. Yet that is the heart and the glory of the teaching of Scripture. It leaves justification short of where Scripture takes it. For justification does not merely take us 'back to square one' as it were. In justification we are not only told that Christ has paid the debt of our sins. We receive Christ's righteousness! We are not simply *like Adam*, beginning all over again; we are *in Christ*. In the sight of God we are not only innocent, but *as righteous as Christ is*, because righteous with his personal righteousness! Dare we believe that? It is what Scripture encourages us to believe and a truth that has brought strong assurance to many:

> *Jesus, Thy blood and righteousness*
> *My beauty are, my glorious dress;*
> *Midst flaming worlds, in these arrayed,*
> *With joy shall I lift up my head.*
>
> *Bold shall I stand in that great day,*
> *For who aught to my charge shall lay?*
> *Fully absolved through Thee I am,*
> *From sin and fear, from guilt and shame.*

> *The holy, meek, unspotted Lamb,*
> *Who from the Father's bosom came,*
> *Who died for me, even me, to atone.*
> *Now for my Lord and God I own.*
>
> *This spotless robe the same appears*
> *When ruined nature sinks in years;*
> *No age can change its glorious hue,*
> *The robe of Christ is ever new.*
>   Nicolaus Ludwig von Zinzendorf
>   tr. by John Wesley

It is this perspective which led us to stress earlier in the chapter that justification is not subject to degrees. It cannot wax and wane. If only we grasped that justification is ours *in Christ*; that we are therefore as truly and finally justified as Christ is; that justification is free and unmerited, we would enjoy an ever deepening sense of peace with God and proceed to rejoice in our hope of sharing his glory (Rom. 5:1–2)!

JUSTIFICATION BY FAITH

God justly justifies sinners because of the work of Christ. Christ is the atoning sacrifice for our sins (1 Jn. 1:9). When we confess our sins we discover that God is *faithful and just* to forgive our sins and cleanse us from our unrighteousness (1 Jn. 2:2). But how does Christ's righteousness become ours? The answer is *by faith in Christ.*

This way of justification appears in the early pages of the Old Testament. In his letters to the Galatians and Romans Paul falls back on the example of Abraham to prove the point. 'Was not Abraham justified by works?' asked many of the Jews, 'and are we not the children of Abraham, following the example of our father?' 'Did he not receive the declaration of righteousness because of what he did to please God?' Paul's answer is an emphatic *no!*

Abraham was not justified by works. Scripture makes it clear that it was because he *believed* God that he was justified (Rom. 4:1–3). It is those who *believe* who are the true children of Abraham (Gal. 3:6–7). Furthermore, Abraham was not justified by the sacrament of circumcision, because Scripture tells us he was circumcised *after*, not *before* he was justified! (Rom. 4:9–12). Did he not receive justification then by obedience to the law? Paul retorts with his trump card: Law brings condemnation, Law shows our sin in its true nature—how then could Abraham have been justified by it? (Rom. 4:15). Furthermore, (as he had already indicated to the Galatians), to suggest such a thing is to display ignorance of the Scriptures! The Law was introduced four hundred and thirty years after Abraham had received God's promise and was justified by faith! In fact the Law was 'added' (Gal. 3:19), it 'came in by the side door' (Rom. 5:19), and was given in order to make men see how necessary dependence on the promise of justification is! How can the Law bring justification when it was given to reveal our condemnation? The Jews (and many after them) not only misunderstand faith (on which they do not rely) but they even misunderstand Law (on which they do rely)! So runs Paul's teaching.

Faith only an instrument

This concentration upon faith should not lead us to think that we are saved because of faith. The Greek text of the New Testament is rich and varied in the ways it describes the relationship between faith and justification. But one expression it never uses. *The New Testament never says that justification is on the basis of, on the grounds of, or because of faith.* (It is misleading of the R.S.V. to translate Romans 3:30 as: 'he will justify the circumcised *on the ground of* their faith.' The same expression is translated 'through faith' in Rom. 1:17.) Faith is never more than the instrument, the channel by which we receive grace and justification. J. C. Ryle expresses the position vividly:

> True faith has *nothing whatever of merit* about it, and in the highest sense cannot be called 'a work'. It is but laying hold of a Saviour's hand, leaning on a husband's arm, and receiving a physician's medicine. It brings with it nothing to Christ but a sinful man's soul. It gives nothing, contributes nothing, pays nothing, performs nothing. It only receives, takes, accepts, grasps, and embraces the glorious gift of justification which Christ bestows, and by renewed daily acts enjoys that gift.
>
> *Old Paths*, p. 228

This is exactly the point that Paul seems to be making in Romans 4:16. He says, 'the promise comes by faith, so that it may be by grace and may be guaranteed ...' Faith means dependence on another and not on oneself. It therefore locks in to the principle of grace. But further, the principle of grace destroys the false principle of works. They are different and opposite ways of coming to God, as Paul demonstrates in Romans 4. If a man is justified by grace, it is impossible that he should be justified by works.

Faith silences boasting

A further affirmation can now be made: if justification is by grace, then there can be no room for boasting before God. This is the point of the rather striking statement Paul makes when he asks: 'Where then is boasting? It is excluded. On what principle? On that of observing the law? No, but on that of faith' (Rom. 3:27). If justification is by faith, then it must be by grace. If it is by grace, then it is unmerited, and boasting ceases.

Faith implies a guarantee

Paul has one final emphasis. Justification is *of* grace to be received as a gift *by* faith in order that God may *guarantee* his promise of salvation. If justification depended on works, it would be unobtainable. Even if it were obtainable it would be subject to decay unless a man were able to continue to justify himself by his works. Thank God this is not the case! Justification is all of grace. It is based on the work of Christ not on our works. God is able therefore to *guarantee* it to us. It is ours by guarantee of a God who never lies, whose gifts and calling are irrevocable (Rom. 11:29).

The man who knows he is justified is a man of unbounded confidence and assurance. He knows that none of his failures can ever change the divine verdict. It is guaranteed and settled for ever in heaven:

> *Other refuge have I none;*
> *Hangs my helpless soul on Thee;*
> *Leave, ah! leave me not alone,*
> *Still support and comfort me:*
> *All my trust on Thee is stayed,*

> *All my help from Thee I bring;*
>   *Cover my defenceless head*
>   *With the shadow of Thy wing.*
>
> *Thou, O Christ, art all I want;*
>   *More than all in Thee I find;*
>   *Raise the fallen, cheer the faint,*
>   *Heal the sick, and lead the blind:*
> *Just and holy is Thy Name,*
>   *I am all unrighteousness;*
> *False and full of sin I am,*
>   *Thou art full of truth and grace.*
>
> *Plenteous grace in Thee is found,*
>   *Grace to cover all my sin;*
> *Let the healing streams abound,*
>   *Make and keep me pure within:*
> *Thou of life the fountain art,*
>   *Freely let me take of Thee;*
> *Spring Thou up within my heart,*
>   *Rise to all eternity.*
>
> Charles Wesley

Can there be anything more amazing than this? In fact there is. The God who justifies us as our Judge now invites us as a Father into his family!

10
Sons of God

Relatively few books have been written on the doctrine of adoption. One written a century ago by a well-known Scottish theologian of his day, Robert S. Candlish, provoked an unusual controversy within the limited confines of Scottish theology. His work was entitled *The Fatherhood of God* and was followed by a series of sermons entitled *The Sonship and Brotherhood of Believers*. But since those days all too little has been written on the subject. The reason is probably that the biblical idea of the Fatherhood of God has been changed into a form of universalism. If we are sons of God by nature where is the need of adoption?

Invariably when a great doctrine is misused there is a tendency for it to be devalued. Thus evangelical preaching has lacked emphasis on Divine Fatherhood and the corresponding experience of sonship because of an unspoken fear of appearing to preach universalism. Other reasons can be found for this unhappy state of affairs. Often in the study of Christian doctrine, adoption or sonship has been treated as virtually the same as either justification or regeneration. It is therefore important to state at the outset that *adoption is not justification, nor is adoption the same thing as regeneration.*

Not justification
Some theologians have spoken of adoption as 'the positive element' in justification. Undoubtedly the New Testament never separates justification and adoption, but neither does it confuse them. In human terms it is quite possible to imagine a man being justified without the remotest thought of his being adopted. The fact that a judge pronounces the verdict of 'not guilty' does not commit him to take the accused to his home and allow him all the privileges of his son! Few men would strive for a place on the bench under those circumstances! Rather the different terminology Scripture uses is intended to enlarge our understanding of the multi-coloured grace of God (1 Pet. 4:10). When the light of the gospel passes through the prism of biblical language we find that it

is broken up into many constituent parts, each with its own beauty and glory. Adoption emphasises an element in our relationship with God which is not present in justification.

Not regeneration

Adoption is not regeneration. The apostles distinguished these things in their writings. The apostle John is the supreme example of this: to those who were '*born* not of natural descent, nor of human decision or a husband's will, but born of God', God '*gave the right* to become children' (Jn. 1:12–13). Here two things are involved in bringing us to sonship. We are born again, and thus given the *nature* of sons, but we are also given an *adoptive right* so that we have a true *status* as sons commensurate with our new nature. This is made a little clearer in 1 John 3:1: 'How great is the love the Father has lavished on us, that we should be *called children* of God! *And that is what we are!*' John's point is—we are called children because adopted; but this is not a title which has no bearing upon our actual experience. It is a title which is matched in our hearts by the work of regeneration. God has done what no human can do—in adopting us he has also given us the nature of our Father (2 Pet. 1:4). But, like justification, adoption is not subject to degrees of more or less. Rather it expresses the new status that God has given us, the experience of which will only be fully known in glory when we will perfectly bear the image of Christ (Rom. 8:19, 23; 1 Jn. 3:2).

Understanding adoption should mean that our own sense of the great goodness and love of God is immeasurably enriched.

The Meaning of Adoption

Adoption or sonship is an exclusively Pauline word although, as we have already noted, the *idea* of being a son is found elsewhere in the New Testament. Paul uses the expression in Galatians 4:5; Ephesians 1:5, and in Romans 8:15, 23; 9:4. But the idea is also present every time we read of the Fatherhood of God. His is the regenerating power which plants the divine seed in our hearts (1 Jn. 3:9). His is the declaration which makes us his sons and daughters.

The background of adoption

Where did this idea of adoption come from? In the family life of the Old Testament no legal provision was made for adoption. Family structures were of such a nature that it was virtually unnecessary. Israel was seen as God's son (e.g. Hos. 11:1 ff). But this was an act of creation on God's part, not of adoption. Even when the Old Testament speaks of the King as God's son, the picture is probably not drawn from this family background.

Adoption in the New Testament is probably to be seen against the background of Roman Law with which the apostle Paul (as a Roman citizen—Acts 22:27-9; 23:27) would be so familiar. In Roman society, unlike our own, the purpose of adoption in law was not to safeguard the rights and privileges of the child but was exclusively thought of in terms of the benefits and blessings which the adopter received. (Of course in our own society adopting parents reap great benefits, and rightly so, but these are never seen to be the main purpose of adoption in which the law is concerned for the child.) There are instances of people benefiting in this way by adopting a person much older than themselves with a view to receiving an inheritance! Adopting someone younger was also seen as a valuable way to guard against the inevitable rigours and burdens of old age! Interestingly Paul uses the idea of adoption exclusively in letters directed to areas under the rule of Roman Law (Galatia, Ephesus and Rome itself). This Roman background serves to remind us that even the highest privileges of the Christian's experience do not have his own happiness as their only goal. They all eventually lead to the honour and glory of God. In the adoption of sons and daughters he restores *for himself* that glory of the image of his Son which was marred and shattered at the Fall.

The Act of Adoption

What then was involved in adoption? There were two basic transactions. The old authority under which the individual stood had to be broken. He was then formally brought under the new authority. Even when the New Testament does not use the language of adoption these ideas appear. The legally established dominion of sin has to be broken. The strength of sin is the law (1 Cor. 15:56). Sin uses it as a fulcrum to lever its way into the life of man (cf. Rom. 5:20; 7:7:13). Sin also claims a legal right to dominion over man because by his disobedience he has forfeited his liberty. That authority of the powers of darkness must be broken if a lasting adoption is to be possible. This God has done in Christ (cf. Rom. 6:1–14). But that is not enough. God inaugurates us into a new relationship with himself by adopting us into his family and bestowing upon us the rights and privileges of true children of God. In fact one of the points which R. S. Candlish daringly affirmed in *The Fatherhood of God* was that the only difference between our enjoyment of sonship and Christ's was that *Christ enjoyed the privileges of sonship before we do, but not in a different manner.* It is not difficult to see why his statement caused so much controversy. What was, and remains difficult to see, is how it can be demonstrated that this is contrary to Scripture! Perhaps Candlish went *beyond* what is written, but it is not easy to show that he went *against* what is written. His motive of raising our eyes to the amazing privileges of our sonship was itself laudable enough:

> *Behold th'amazing gift of love*
> *the Father hath bestow'd*
> *On us, the sinful sons of men,*
> *to call us sons of God!*

THE SIGNIFICANCE OF ADOPTION

In studying justification earlier we saw that the way of salvation in both Old and New Testaments was the same, by grace through faith. Any other interpretation would have disastrous effects on the way we read Scripture and on our understanding of the character of God. But it is possible to understand this unity in such a way that we lose the balance of Scripture. There is a profound difference between the clarity and fulness of revelation and experience in the days of the Old Covenant by contrast with the days of the New Covenant. That difference does not lie either in the *reality* of salvation or in the *way* of salvation (1 Pet. 3:20; Rom. 4:18–25). It lies in the fulness of the experience of grace possible. There is not only *continuity* between the promise in the Old Testament and its fulfilment in

Christ, there is *incalculable increase* of blessing. The believers in the Old Testament could not reach maturity apart from us, says the writer of Hebrews (Heb. 11:40).

One of the ways in which this is seen is *in the division of time* about which the New Testament speaks. In Romans 3:21, after cataloguing the condemning words of God about men's sin, Paul tells us that something new has taken place: '*But now* a righteousness from God ... has been made known' (Rom. 3:21). Through Christ the blessing of God promised to Abraham comes to the Gentiles (Gal. 3:14) and a better covenant with better promises is inaugurated (Heb. 8:6 ff).

But the main distinction lies *in the character of fellowship with God*. Even at their highest the saints in the Old Testament never rose to a settled personal relationship to God defined and enjoyed in terms of individual sonship and personal Fatherhood. Scholars have often pointed out the novelty and uniqueness of Jesus' teaching precisely here. It is this that characterises the advance in experience of the new era, and leads to the summit of spiritual experience. Think of the privilege of calling the Creator of the ends of the earth, 'Abba, Father'. It defies comprehension and calculation. That is why there are few pictures more moving than the application of Isaiah 8:18 to Jesus in Hebrews 2:13. There he is pictured among the worshipping people of God, as the leader of their worship. He extends his hands towards his Father. He sings God's praise and rejoices in the fellowship of his people, saying: 'Here am I, and the children God has given me.'

This fellowship is the fruit of the ministry of the Spirit as well as of the work of Christ. When Jesus speaks about 'streams of living water', John adds, 'By this he meant the Spirit, whom those who believed in him were *later to* receive. Up to that time the Spirit had not been given, since Jesus had not yet been glorified' (Jn. 7:38–9). All translations convey John's meaning, but they do not often succeed in conveying the strength of his expression. For his words literally read: 'Up to that time the Spirit *was not*.' Naturally, John does not mean to suggest the non-existence of the Spirit (cf. Jn 1:32–4). What he emphasises is the radical distinction between those days in our Lord's ministry and the day of the Spirit which was yet to be. Later in the Gospel the significance of this is drawn out more fully. When

Jesus leaves the disciples, he will not leave them 'desolate' (Jn. 14:18 R.S.V.). The Greek word is *orphanos*, and N.I.V. rightly translates it as 'orphans'. What the disciples are learning is that when God's Spirit comes, he will come in all the grace of Jesus himself. But he will come also as the One who will bring them a consciousness that they have a Father in heaven who cares for them. What Jesus had taught in the Sermon on the Mount about the Fatherhood of God they will now discover in their experience through the ministry of the Spirit (cf. Matt. 6:5–14, 25–32). Just as Jesus uniquely spoke of God as his Father, so when the Spirit of Jesus comes to abide for ever in the hearts of the disciples, they will know in a totally new way what it is to cry, '*Abba*, Father' (Rom. 8:15).

In fact, we do not rightly understand what a privilege adoption is until we have some appreciation of the ministry of the Spirit as 'the Spirit of adoption'.

THE SPIRIT OF ADOPTION

In two places Paul speaks of the special relationship between the Spirit and our experience of adoption. In Galatians 4:1–7, he describes the new thing God has done in bringing into being the new covenant. In Romans 8:12–27, he speaks of the personal experience of the Spirit as the Spirit of adoption:

> those who are led by the Spirit of God are sons of God. For you did not receive a spirit that makes you a slave again to fear, but you received the Spirit of sonship [adoption]. And by him we cry, '*Abba*, Father'. The Spirit himself testifies with our spirit that we are God's children ...

The Romans had already known a 'spirit that makes you a slave again to fear'. Paul is probably speaking of the days when they were conscious of the deep conviction of sin which made them realise their bondage and engendered a feeling of terror at their condition. But through the gospel this has been dispelled and they have received the Spirit of sonship. They have now entered into the blood-bought privileges of brotherhood to Christ and sonship to God.

Marks of the Spirit's presence

There are four marks of the presence of this Spirit in adoption.

(i) *We are led by the Spirit of God* (Rom. 8:14). Just as a Father provides guidelines for his children (and in a sense they may find the spirit of their father is the determining factor in many of their characteristic responses to life-situations), so in a much more profound sense the Spirit of God is the guide of the children of God: 'those who are led by the Spirit of God are sons of God' (Rom. 8:14). But the leading of which Paul speaks has a very clear and definite content here. It is connected intimately with the help the Spirit is said to give in verse 13, to 'put to death the misdeeds of the body'. *The guidance the Spirit provides is that of clear-cut opposition to sin.* To claim to experience the ministry of the Spirit of adoption and yet to dally with sin is to be utterly deceived. The Spirit of adoption is the same Person as the Spirit of holiness of whom Paul had earlier spoken (Rom. 1:4). *His presence brings a new attitude to sin.* Where that new attitude is present, he is present.

(ii) *We cry 'Abba, Father'* (Rom. 8:15). This is a point at which widespread misunderstanding has arisen. It is sometimes suggested that the evidence of the presence of the Spirit of adoption and the assurance he brings will be a spirit of tranquil resting in the presence of God. No doubt there is such blessing brought to us by the Spirit of God. But it is not such an experience that is being described in Romans 8:15. Paul speaks here about the Christian *crying* '*Abba*, Father!' The verb he uses is *krazein*, and in the New Testament it denotes a loud cry, often a cry or shriek of anguish (cf. Mk. 15:39, our Lord's cry on the Cross; Rev. 12:2, a woman in childbirth). The picture is not that of the believer resting quietly in his Father's arms in child-like faith, but of the child who has tripped and fallen crying out in pain, 'Daddy, Daddy'. *That* cry is the mark of the presence of the Spirit of adoption, not least because it shows that in time of need it is towards our Father in heaven that we look.

(iii) *The witness of the Spirit* (Rom. 8:16) is one of the most difficult phrases of all rightly to interpret, and yet there is a measure of truth in John Wesley's father's exhortation to him to seek it as 'the real proof of Christianity'. Often it has been interpreted as a mystical inner voice which speaks comfort and assurance to the believer. By others it is understood as referring to the testimony of Scripture in which alone the Spirit of God speaks to man. It seems best to understand Paul to mean that this co-witness of the Spirit appears *in our experience of the other evidences of sonship*, namely mortification of the sin which would displease our Father, and application to his Fatherly care in times of need. In these very experiences, Paul is saying, the Spirit is actively confirming us in our sense of sonship.

(iv) *The Spirit of adoption indwelling us means that in this life the believer groans!* (Rom. 8:23). Not only does creation groan (v. 22) and the Spirit himself apparently groans (v. 26), but we ourselves groan. This is not the groaning of the believer in his struggle to mortify sin as in verse 13. 'The 'groans' of Romans 8 are more prospective than present. The creation 'groans' as it looks forward to a future liberty; the Spirit groans as he looks forward to his ministry producing answered prayer; the believer groans for an ever fuller experience of salvation.

We can honestly sing with Isaac Watts:

> *The men of grace have found*
> *Glory begun below;*
> *Celestial fruit on earthly ground*
> *From faith and hope may grow.*

We enjoy this great salvation now, through the Spirit. But the Spirit 'is a deposit guaranteeing our inheritance until the redemption of those who are God's possession' (Eph. 1:14 cf. Rom. 8:23). We do not experience 'full salvation' here and now. So we 'groan' longing for the day when we will drink to the full of the rivers of living water which we have already begun to taste.

Only in so far as we have a measure of this experience do we know what it is consciously to sense that we are children of God and enjoy the ministry of 'the Spirit of adoption'. When we do we also discover that being God's children brings responsibilities as well as privileges.

PRIVILEGES AND RESPONSIBILITIES

(i) A new status

We now belong to the family of God in all ages and from every nation under the sun. There is nothing like this fellowship in human society. We are given a new name, as sons of God, and are not children of the devil (1 Jn. 3:10), or sons of disobedience (Eph. 5:6), or children destined for wrath (Eph. 2:3). On the contrary we have extended to us the privileges and pleasures of our Father's home—access to his presence, familiarity with him (which basically means 'belonging to the same family'), boldness and liberty to come to him, and a knowledge that his Fatherly hand will work all things together for the good of all his children.

The corresponding *responsibility* is to become like him, and in particular to emulate his love for all his children and therefore treat our fellow-Christians with love and affection, with openheartedness and tender devotion. The recognition that we have brothers and sisters in Christ, objects of *his love* as we ourselves are, should stimulate a deep personal care for them. How easily we lose sight of that!

(ii) A new sense of God's care

We meditate too little on the profound truth expressed so simply by Jesus: 'Your Father knows what you need before you ask him' (Matt. 6:8). How long it took Peter before he was able to pass this word on out of personal experience! Yet eventually he was able to encourage every generation of Christians with his exhortation: 'Cast all your anxiety upon him because he cares for you' (1 Pet. 5:7).

Our *responsibility* is therefore to lay aside all our anxieties. We must *bring them* to our Father, and, assured of his care, *leave them* with him.

(iii) A new sense of destiny

Our ultimate privilege lies in the future, for although we already experience our inheritance as joint-heirs with Christ, there is more yet to come! Thus Paul relates the thought of adoption into God's family to the whole chain of God's saving activity which will only be completed in glory (Eph. 1:5, 11, 14). The *responsibility* of such a prospect is clearly marked out for us: 'Everyone who has this hope in him purifies himself, just as he [Christ] is pure' (1 Jn. 3:3). To know that we are God's adopted children is to be constrained to exhibit his character, since one day we will live forever in his home. If that is so, we should be willing to share the pattern of life of Christ our Elder Brother, for

> if we are children, then we are heirs—heirs of God and co-heirs with Christ, if indeed we share in his sufferings in order that we may also share in his glory.
>
> Romans 8:17

If we endure,
we will also reign with him.

2 Timothy 2:12

11
Union with Christ

These studies have concentrated attention on what it means to be brought into the family of God. One of our great needs as Christians is to catch a vision of this, and to see our new life in Christ as the glorious and dignified thing that it really is. The great temptation most of us face is to believe that very little has happened to us through grace. We still stumble and fall far short of the high calling which is ours in Christ. Scripture encourages us to hold a different perspective by enlarging our understanding of what God has done for us, and has begun to accomplish in us.

In this context we must consider a doctrine which lies at the heart of the Christian life, and is intimately related to all the other doctrines we have so far considered. It is the link joining them all together in one harmonious whole. The truth to which the New Testament constantly returns is that as Christians we are *united to Christ*.

IN CHRIST

Union with Christ is frequently described as our being 'in Christ'. Paul calls his readers 'saints', people set apart by and for God, and he invariably addresses them as those who are 'in Christ' or 'in Christ Jesus' (1 Cor. 1:2; Eph. 1:1; Phil. 1:1; Col. 1:1; 1 Thess. 1:1; 2 Thess. 1:1). Parallel to this is another emphasis—Christ is 'in' the believer (cf. Rom. 8:10; Gal. 2:20; Col. 1:27). These expressions indicate the closeness of the bond between our Lord and his people. This is one of the great 'mysteries' which has been revealed in the gospel (Col. 1:27). It is something which God makes known only through revelation.

Union with Christ is the foundation of all our spiritual experience and all spiritual blessings. These are given to us 'in Christ', and only those who are 'in Christ' ever experience them. Paul emphasises this particularly in Ephesians 1:3-14 which we previously discussed in connection with the plan of salvation in chapter 2. In the Greek text these twelve verses are in fact one long sentence! Paul is so caught up in his sense of the great blessings of the gospel that he hardly has time to pause for breath. We have been *'blessed'* in Christ, he says, just as we have been *chosen* (v. 4), *graced* (v. 6), *redeemed* (v. 7), *reconciled* (v. 10), *destined* (v. 11) and *sealed* (v. 13) in Christ. From beginning to end the Christian life is Christ-centred and we are constantly to look to him for all the spiritual provision we need. All spiritual blessings are in him, and it is only as we ourselves, in this Pauline sense, are 'in Christ' that we will find the blessings which are ours in Christ becoming realities in our own experience.

The Background

How did this idea of union with Christ become such a central part of Paul's theology? There was a time when many scholars argued that Paul had taken the idea over from pagan 'mystery' religions, and employed it for his own purpose. But in view of Paul's strong inclination to see Christ and his work against an Old Testament background it would be a rash approach to look beyond that for a source *if* an adequate background could be found within the pages of Scripture itself. There is no doubt that such a background can readily be discerned.

For one thing, the idea of union and communion lies at the heart of the Old Testament's view of God's relationship with his people. One of the pictures which expresses this is that of marriage. God's covenant with his people is paralleled with the marriage bond and interpreted in the light of it. This is the background to one of the most moving sections of Isaiah in which the prophet speaks of Israel's Maker as a husband who proves his faithfulness in the midst of her unfaithfulness (Is. 54:5-8). Jeremiah speaks of God as his people's husband (Jer. 31:32), and the book of Hosea is built upon this concept.

The Old Testament is also familiar with the idea of representative or 'corporate' personality in which one person takes the place of many others and the many are seen to be united together in the accomplishments of the one. They share in his gains or losses. The principle involved is vividly illustrated in the story of David and Goliath (1 Sam. 17) in which the victory of young David was obviously interpreted in corporate rather than individual terms. His victory was the victory of his people, and the basis on which they pursued and defeated the Philistines (1 Sam. 17:51). Other figures in the Old Testament illustrate this same representative principle, so that what they achieve may then belong to those in whose place they stand. Thus the figure of the Son of Man in Daniel 7:13-14, 22 has both an individual and a corporate dimension. In the regulation of the sacrificial system, the High Priest sacrifices and prays as the representative of the whole people. The people had a share in all he did for them. In the Servant Songs in Isaiah (chs. 42; 49; 50; 52-3) the righteous *one* carries the sins of the *many*, and what he accomplishes belongs to them because of the bond between the Servant and the 'many'.

In the New Testament this teaching is given more explicit form in the Gospel of John. In the Upper Room Jesus seems to focus his teaching increasingly on this central issue, and when he opens his heart in prayer to the Father in John 17, this union which he has established between himself and his disciples is eloquently expressed. He speaks of the disciples' union with one another being as close as his own union with his Father, because based on their union with him (17:23, 26). In the light of his earlier illustration of the vine and the branches (Jn. 15:1-11) it is beyond dispute that here we have a central burden in Christ's teaching of his own disciples. Just as a shoot is grafted into the vine and receives its nourishment from the vine, so the disciple is 'in Christ' and draws from Christ all spiritual benefits.

Paul takes up these earlier hints and develops them in the letters. In fact what we have in his teaching is an outworking of the initial revelation of Christ to him on the road to Damascus. There Jesus revealed himself to Paul precisely in terms of his union with his own people; to Saul who persecuted only Christians (as he thought) the Lord said, 'Saul, Saul, why do you persecute *me*' (Acts 9:5; cf. 22:8; 26:14). It was Jesus whom Saul was persecuting—because of the mysterious union established between himself and the church. Later in his writings, Paul uses various images to try to express the power of this spiritual truth, such as the marriage union (Eph. 5:32) or the relationship of head and body (Eph. 4:15-16). He teaches that every believer is united to Christ, is 'in Christ'. But what exactly is the nature of this union, and what are its dimensions?

The Nature of Union with Christ

This union is sometimes referred to as 'the mystical union'. The term is not a biblical one and may be too broad a term adequately to clarify our understanding of what it means to be 'in Christ'. Often 'mystical' suggests the idea of a merging between oneself and God. But union with Christ should not be thought of in terms of a loss of our own identity.

We may find some help in understanding our union with Christ if we think of it in terms of the following categories:

(i) A federal union

Federal comes from the Latin *foedus*, meaning a treaty or covenant. What is being emphasised here is that God has established a relationship between Christ and his people which may be thought of as a covenant. What Christ does becomes theirs by virtue of union with him.

Theologians used to speak about a 'Covenant of Works' in which all men were united to Adam as their representative, and therefore fell in his transgression (Rom. 5:12-21). Paul saw the parallel to that in the relationship of Christ to his people. Christ appeared as 'Adam in reverse', undoing what Adam did, regaining what Adam lost, restoring to man what was forfeited by Adam. So Paul says that through Christ's obedience, on the basis of this covenant relationship between him and ourselves, grace abounds over our sin, justification becomes a reality, and believers reign in life. All this is because of one man's act of righteousness (Rom. 5:18-19). But that is only possible if there is this objective union between Jesus and ourselves.

The federal union is effected *outside of us* and *in Christ*.

(ii) A carnal or flesh union

By his incarnation the Son of God became one with us, sharing our nature. He came 'made in human likeness' (Phil. 2:7), 'in the likeness of the flesh of sin' (Rom. 8:3). These are difficult words to interpret, but they appear to suggest that in his conception Christ really took hold of our nature in the womb of the virgin Mary, sanctified it through the Spirit, and lived out his life of obedience *in the weakness of our flesh*. He came truly to brother us, and to be tempted in all points as we are so that he might sympathise with us in our weakness (Heb. 4:15). Furthermore, he established this bridge between God and us in our flesh in order that he might come into contact with our sin, being 'made sin' for us (2 Cor. 5:21). We are united to him by divine covenant and also by divine incarnation. Our union with Christ is therefore based on Christ's union with us.

(iii) A faith union

Faith not only rests upon Christ, but, according to the language of the New Testament, brings us 'into' Christ. On some fifty occasions we read of believing 'into' him (e.g. Jn. 2:11; 3:16; Rom. 10:14; Gal. 2:16; Phil. 1:29). All spiritual blessings are ours *in Christ*, but only when we get into Christ will they be of practical benefit to us.

How then do we get 'into Christ'? The Scriptures reply, *by faith*. The significance of this is sometimes overlooked in our popular preaching and teaching, in that it emphasises the need for a man to get *out of himself* and into Christ. Occasionally the New Testament speaks of becoming a Christian in terms of receiving Christ, and thus *getting Christ into our lives*. But the emphasis is on *the need to be taken out of ourselves* and our sin, and be 'found in Christ'. That gives union to Christ a very important practical dimension. It is not to be thought of primarily as a subjective experience which encourages us to look *in* and *down*. Rather it is something which lifts us *up* and *out*, and draws us on to the glorious liberty of the children of God. So in the allegory of the Vine and the branches (Jn. 15:1 ff) the chief need of the 'branch' or 'shoot' is to be grafted into the Vine to depend entirely upon its nourishment.

(iv) A spiritual union

Perhaps this seems so obvious that it is scarcely worth saying. But what it essentially means is that our union with the Lord is created by the agency of the Holy Spirit. He carries us 'into Christ'. Paul indicates the closeness of this union in 1 Corinthians 6:17: 'But he who unites himself with the Lord is one with him in spirit.'

(v) An extensive union

It extends to Christ in his total human experience. Paul makes considerable use of this argument:

If we are united to Christ
Then we are united to him in all he has done for us.

Passages such as Romans 6:1 ff; Galatians 2:20; Colossians 2:20–3:4 together indicate how far-reaching this is. If we are united to Christ, we share in his life, death, burial, resurrection, ascension, hidden session in glory and will also share in his return. So extensive is this union that Paul can say that Christ 'is our life' (Col. 3:4). So Wesley's words are profoundly true:

Soar we now where Christ has led,
Following our exalted Head;
Made like Him, like Him we rise:
Ours the Cross, the grave, the skies.
Hail the Lord of earth and heaven!
Praise to Thee by both be given;
Thee we greet triumphant now;
Hail, the Resurrection Thou!

In the light of such an extensive union, we may well wonder whether Wesley means that *we* greet *the triumphant Christ*, or whether *we in triumph* come to greet him to whom we are everlastingly united!

(vi) A union of life

Paul emphasises in these same passages just quoted that the fruit of our union with Jesus is always life. This is why we have been grafted into the Vine, in order that the life of the Vine might become clearly visible in our lives. It is no longer we who live, but Christ who lives in us. The life we now live is *through faith in the Son of God* who has loved us and given himself for us (Gal. 2:20).

It may be asked in response to these dimensions of our fellowship in Christ: *Surely we must be many years on the road with Christ before we are the recipients of all of these dimensions?* But this is to misunderstand! These are not benefits to which faith works up, but blessings which are bestowed upon us the moment we belong to Christ. If we are Christians, all of this is true of all of us all of the time! When Christ became ours, he became ours in his entirety in order to work in us a full salvation. It is this which is the ultimate purpose of the union which we have been describing.

Transformation

We have seen that through union with Christ all that is his by incarnation becomes ours through faith. His self-offering becomes ours to bring us pardon for our guilt; his life of obedience becomes ours to give us the new status of sons of God. But when we are joined to him there is also a sense in which his life and power become available to us to transform our lives. We may even go so far as to say that when we are united to Christ the whole of his past life is made available to us, not simply to compensate for our past (by way of pardon) but actually to sanctify our present lives, so that our own past may not inescapably *dominate* our present Christian life. We, who in the past have marred the image of God by sin, may gaze into the face of Christ and discover power and holiness there on which to draw so that the power of our own past sin may not destroy us in the present. Thus, in more general terms, Louis Berkhof has put it like this:

> By this union believers are changed into the image of Christ *according to his human nature*. What Christ effects in his people is in a sense a replica or reproduction of what took place with him. Not only objectively, but in a subjective sense also they bear the cross, are crucified, die, and are raised to newness of life with Christ. They share in a measure in the experiences of their Lord, Matt. 16:24; Rom. 6:5; Gal. 2:20; Col. 1:23; 2:12; 3:1; 1 Pet. 4:13.
>
> *Systematic Theology*, p. 451

The cost

The implications of this are very far-reaching. Union with Christ involves sharing in and with Christ, and that implies commitment to him principally as a crucified and risen Lord. During his own ministry this was the central emphasis in his preaching. If any man is to be his disciple he must take up the

Cross daily and follow him (Matt. 16:24; Mk. 8:34; Lk. 9:23). Every genuine expression of the Christian life has recognised this. But perhaps it has never been more eloquently expressed than in the words of Dietrich Bonhoeffer:

> The cross is laid on every Christian. The first Christ-suffering which every man must experience is the call to abandon the attachments of this world. It is that dying of the old man which is the result of his encounter with Christ. As we embark upon discipleship we surrender ourselves to Christ in union with his death—we give our lives to death. Thus it begins; the cross is not the terrible end to an otherwise godfearing and happy life, but it meets us at the beginning of our communion with Christ. When Christ calls a man, he bids him come and die.
>
> *The Cost of Discipleship*, p. 79

In other words, the privilege of being united to a risen and ascended Christ, who showers upon us the multitude of spiritual blessings we enjoy, has *one* condition. It cannot be separated from belonging to the crucified Christ, and sharing in the death we must die with him to self and the world. Paul points us to this in his letter to the Galatians when he emphasises three things about the Cross. *On* it Christ was crucified. *Through it* the world is crucified to us. *Because of it* we will be crucified to the world (Gal. 6:14). It is as we enter more deeply into this fellowship with Christ that our lives bear spiritual fruit. So Paul described his share in Christ's sufferings: he was hard pressed; he was perplexed; he was persecuted; he was struck down (2 Cor. 4:8–9). What was the explanation? 'We always carry around in our body the death of Jesus, so that the life of Jesus may also be revealed in our body. For we who are alive are always being given over to death for Jesus' sake, so that his life may be revealed in our mortal body. So then, *death is at work in us, but life is at work in you*' (2 Cor. 4:10–12). By such means Paul knew the power of Christ's resurrection and shared in the fellowship of his sufferings (Phil. 3:10).

The fruit

On the other side of the Cross lay the Resurrection. That pattern is invariable. Through union with Christ in his death comes union with him in his resurrection and a share in his triumph. The power by which he was raised from the dead is the power by which he works in us (Eph. 1:18–21). If this is so it is not at all surprising that Paul is able to speak about the glorious victory of the Christian (Rom. 8:37). We experience it in a whole variety of ways:

(i) The knowledge of our union with Christ *provides us with great dignity*. As I look at myself I see failure, sin, sometimes shame and disgrace. But that is neither the ultimate nor the whole truth about me as a Christian. No! I am united to Christ, a joint-heir of his riches, a child of God. Knowing this to be the real truth about me lends grace and power to my life.

(ii) The knowledge of our union with Christ also *gives us confidence in prayer*. It was when Jesus had begun to expound the closeness of this union that he also began to introduce the disciples to the true heart of prayer. It is as Christ abides in us and we abide in him, as his word dwells in us, and we pray in his name, that God hears us (Jn. 15:4–7). But all of these expressions are simply extensions of the one fundamental idea: If I am united to Christ, then all that is his is mine. So long as my heart, will and mind are one with Christ's in his word, I can approach God with the humble confidence that my prayers will be heard and answered.

(iii) The knowledge of our union with Christ *protects us in temptation*. When we realise who we are, children of God, men and women united to Christ, we have in our possession one of the strongest pieces of armour to fight against the temptations and allurements of the world and the flesh: 'How can I, who am united to the Lord Jesus Christ, give way to this temptation?' If Joseph, tempted by Potiphar's wife, was able to resist her advances by saying: 'No-one is greater in this house than I am. My master has withheld nothing from me ... How then could I do such a wicked thing and sin against God?' and this was defence enough against repeated onslaught (Gen. 39:9–10), how much more powerful is the protest: 'I am united to the Lord Jesus Christ, how can I, of all people, commit this sin?'

This is the very point Paul makes to the Corinthians in dealing with a particularly unseemly sin: 'Do you not realise that you are dragging Christ into your sin?' (1 Cor. 6:15–20). The reminder of what we have become by grace is a constant defence against slipping back into what we were by nature.

Of all the doctrines surrounding the Christian life this, the profoundest, is also the most practical in its effects. It may come as a surprise to learn that, in the New Testament, the doctrine of *Election* is no less practical. In the next chapter we will discover why this is so.

12
Election

In his famous children's book *The Lion, the Witch and the Wardrobe,* C. S. Lewis pictures a mysterious animal world held in the merciless grip of the White Witch of Narnia. She has cast a spell across the land which has the unhappy effect of making it always Winter but never Christmas. Only when Aslan the Lion and Saviour-King appears and sacrifices himself does it emerge that there is a stronger power than that of the Witch. There is what Lewis calls 'Deeper Magic from before the Dawn of Time'. That 'magic' is explained when Aslan comes to life again after his self-sacrifice:

> 'But what does it all mean?' asked Susan when they were somewhat calmer.
> 'It means,' said Aslan, 'that though the Witch knew the Deep Magic, there is a magic deeper still which she did not know. Her knowledge goes back only to the dawn of time. But if she could have looked a little further back, into the stillness and the darkness before time dawned, she would have read there a different incantation. She would have known that when a willing victim who had committed no treachery was killed in a traitor's stead, the Table would crack and Death itself would start working backwards...'
> *The Lion, the Witch & the Wardrobe*, p. 148

But it is not only in the world of Narnia that 'Deeper Magic from before the Dawn of Time' operates. For in Scripture we discover that eternal love and power is at work for our salvation. Our Lion King is a Lamb slain, as it were, from the foundation of the world (Rev. 13:8). In him the secret purposes of God from eternity are revealed (Eph. 3:2–6). He is the elect of God (Is. 42:1). His life was a revelation of the electing purposes of God. Everything that happened to him did so because of divine predestination (Acts 2:23; 4:28). There was 'Deeper Magic from before the Dawn of Time' operative in the ministry of Christ, if we may borrow Lewis's metaphor.

When we begin to think about the biblical doctrines of election and predestination in this light, we will feel some measure of the thrill which the writers oof the New Testament did whenever they wrote about it. For them these truths were not controversial but joyful. They saw that if they were united to Christ, this meant that in choosing Christ and loving him God had also chosen them!

Biblical vocabulary. The words 'predestination' and 'election' are often used as though they were synonyms. It is certainly true that both refer to the same doctrine, but they convey slightly different ideas. To elect means to make a choice. To predestinate emphasises the goal of the choice (Acts 4:28; Rom. 8:28–9; 1 Cor. 2:7; Eph. 1:5–11). In brief, election reflects God's choice of his people, predestination their divinely ordained destiny.

God's Chosen People

In the Old Testament the ideas of election and predestination play a major role and provide one of the basic themes of Old Testament theology. The history of the Jewish nation is seen as the story of the 'chosen people'. Their very existence depends upon the choice of God.

Right from the very beginning of Genesis God reveals his sovereign purpose of salvation (Gen. 3:15; 12:3; 18:18; 22:18; 26:4; 28:14). In pursuit of this revealed plan God chooses men, families, and eventually a whole nation to be the recipients and the bearers of his promise of salvation. From those early stages of divine revelation God had chosen men out of the world to be his servants and evangelists. In Genesis 9:25–6 God chose to work through one segment of Noah's family line rather than the others. In the later chapters his choice takes it centre in Abraham and descends through his family. Then, as the people come into being as a divinely created theocracy in the Exodus, there is repeated emphasis that their existence depends upon the sovereign choice of God (cf. Ex. 20:2; 34:6–7). Later on, both in the Law and the Prophets Israel is warned that she is the *object* and *not the cause* of God's favour:

> Because he loved your forefathers and chose their descendants after them, he brought you out of Egypt by his Presence and his great strength.
>
> Deuteronomy 4:37

> The Lord did not set his affection on you and choose you because you were more numerous than other peoples, for you were the fewest of all peoples. But it was because the Lord loved you and kept the oath he swore to your forefathers that he brought you out with a mighty hand and redeemed you from the land of slavery.
>
> Deuteronomy 7:7–8

> After the Lord your God has driven them out before you, do not say to yourself, 'The Lord has brought me here to take possession of this land because of my righteousness.' ... Understand, then, that it is not because of your righteousness that the Lord your God is giving you this good land to possess, for you are a stiff-necked people.
>
> Deuteronomy 9:4, 6

On this biblical basis the prophets set forth their case against the distortion of divine election which later appeared when the people failed to grasp the principle that privilege brings corresponding responsibility.

Jesus and Election

Jesus taught the doctrine of election. He told men that his Father worked in men's lives on the basis of a plan and purpose. That thought underlies a good deal of his teaching on the kingdom of God. It has already been prepared for the 'blessed' from the foundation of the world (Matt. 25:34). It lies in the Father's hands to bestow the places of honour in that kingdom (Matt. 20:23). These verses give a general indication of the sovereign purposes of God. But Jesus also insists that entry into the kingdom of God is by a call (Matt. 9:13) and that this call is not effectual without a further restraint on the heart on the part of God, in which his choice is put into operation. Many are called (invited—N.I.V.) but few are chosen (Matt. 22:14). The 'comfortable words' are themselves based upon this principle:

> At that time Jesus said, 'I praise you, Father, Lord of heaven and earth, because you have hidden these things from the wise and learned, and revealed them to little children. Yes, Father, for this was your good pleasure.

'All things have been committed to me by my Father. No-one knows the Son except the Father, and no-one knows the Father except the Son and those to whom the Son chooses to reveal him.

'Come to me, all you who are weary and burdened, and I will give you rest...'

Matthew 11:25-28

These words are unfathomable. They take us into the deep things of God, speaking as they do of the inter-personal relationships of the Father and the Son. They point to mysteries beyond our understanding. But they also speak plainly about how men come to know God in Christ. It is *by the choice of the Father and the Son*:

> *Chosen not for good in me,*
> *Wakened up from wrath to flee,*
> *Hidden in the Saviour's side,*
> *By the Spirit sanctified,*
> *Teach me, Lord, on earth to show,*
> *By my love, how much I owe.*
>
> Robert Murray M'Cheyne

Yet it was to put into effect these electing purposes that Christ told his parables. Through them, he maintained, the elect would be called and the self-righteously indifferent would be hardened (Matt. 13:14-15).

The same truth comes out even more forcefully in John's Gospel. Here Jesus shares his deep awareness of the Father's predestined purposes for his own life. He lives by the will of his Father (Jn. 4:34; 5:30; 6:38, 39, 40). He lives for the 'hour' which his Father has already appointed (Jn. 2:4; 7:30; 8:20; 12:27; 13:1; 17:1). Jesus himself was conscious of, and gave expression to the fact that he was under the predestining purposes of God.

But in John's Gospel, Jesus is also seen as the Saviour *of the world*. There is a universal dimension to his mission insofar as he is God's only Son and therefore man's only Saviour. As such he is to be lifted up for all men to see (cf. Jn. 3:16; 5:31; 12:47; 17:21). But this should not blind us to the other emphasis which John portrays without any hint of embarrassment. For throughout the Gospel there is a strand of teaching emphasising election. It appears first of all at a particularly crucial point in the narrative, and its importance is emphasised by the way Jesus' teaching leads to a loss of support among the people:

> Then Jesus declared, 'I am the bread of life. He who comes to me will never go hungry, and he who believes in me will never be thirsty. But as I told you, you have seen me and still you do not believe. All that the Father gives me will come to me, and whoever comes to me I will never drive away. For I have come down from heaven not to do my will but to do the will of him who sent me, that I shall lose none of all that he has given me, but raise them up at the last day. For my Father's will is that everyone who looks to the Son and believes in him shall have eternal life, and I will raise him up at the last day....'
> From this time many of his disciples turned back and no longer followed him.
> John 6:35-40; 66

When men and women come to put their trust in Christ it is not merely as a result of their own will, but takes place in terms of the divine will. Jesus teaches that all those who have been gifted to him by his Father *will come* to him, but also that there is *no other way to come to him*. We cannot ignore this thorough emphasis on God's election. He chooses all those who become his children. Jesus speaks of them as his 'own' (Jn. 6:44; 13:1), the ones he has chosen (13:18; 15:16, 19). For them he prays (17:9), and to them he grants eternal life (10:28; 17:2). What therefore Jesus says primarily of his first disciples can be generalised for all Christians: 'You did not choose me, but I chose you to go and bear fruit' (Jn. 15:16). Privilege brings responsibility.

Paul's Teaching

We have seen enough in the teaching of Jesus not to be deceived by the old criticism that Jesus taught the simple gospel while Paul complicated it with his theological emphases! While it is true that Paul had a strong sense of divine sovereignty and of the electing love of God, it was no stronger than that of the Lord Jesus Christ, nor is it really any more starkly expressed.

According to Paul, God does everything in accordance with his good pleasure (1 Cor. 12:18; 15:38; Eph. 1:11, cf. 1 Cor. 8:6; Rom. 11:36). God has universal rights over his sinful creatures and may use them as he wills for his own glory (Rom. 9:22). Three passages are of supreme significance:

(i) Romans 8:28 ff

Here, as elsewhere in Scripture, predestination is seen in the context of encouraging the hard-pressed and potentially downhearted. Your encouragement in the midst of afflictions, Paul teaches, is that in and through them God is working his perfect purposes out. Rather than impede his plan, these events will be caught up into it and one day will be seen to have been an integral part of it. God works all things together for good for his children (Rom. 8:28). This 'we know'. But how do we know it? Paul's answer is that the purpose of God is immutable, and he records for us the major stages of its outworking in the lives of all believers. There are five listed, Foreknowledge, Predestination, Calling, Justification and Glorification. The first two are of special interest in this chapter. Paul uses the past tense throughout when he speaks of these activities of God, and seems to regard them as accomplished facts. Furthermore these terms are co-extensive with one another in the breadth of their application. We might paraphrase by saying: All whom he foreknew, he predestined; all he predestined he called; all whom he called he justified; all those he justified he also glorified. To be foreknown is, in embryo, to be predestined, called, justified, glorified! *How then are foreknowledge and predestination to be understood?*

The verb 'to foreknow' (*proginōskō*) is used in two different ways in the New Testament. When used in connection with things or facts it means—to know or have information beforehand. It is used in this sense in Acts 26:5; 2 Peter 3:17. When used in connection with people, it has a different sense (Rom. 8:29; 11:2; 1 Pet. 1:20). There it takes on a strong Hebraic sense of 'know', meaning an intimate knowledge and communion with a person rather than mere knowledge of the facts about them. In this sense foreknowledge is really an equivalent of *fore-love* or even of *elect*. This sense of 'love' or 'have intimate fellowship with' is required, for example, in Jesus' words in the Sermon on the Mount. On the Last Day he will tell men who have claimed his power to depart from him because he never 'knew' them. There Jesus must be thinking of fellowship and not of factual information.

What then do we conclude about these words of the apostle? Primarily that he sees the fountain of predestination in the loving heart of God, and that the beat of his heart towards us began before we were ever born. More than this it may be possible to learn from Scripture. Less than this we cannot hold and still have a view of salvation which is fully biblical. Foreknowledge *means* love, *means* election!

(ii) Romans 9–11

In the letter to the Romans Paul is expounding the doctrine of justification. In chapters 1–8 he demonstrates its necessity because of man's sin, expounds its provision in the righteousness of God, and its application in the sanctification of the believer.

In chapters 9–11 he describes its rejection by God's own people the Jews. In chapter 9 Paul defends and justifies the activity of God, in chapter 10 he indicates the way in which the Jews have disqualified themselves from the privileges of the kingdom of God through unbelief. In chapter 11 he expounds the riches of the grace of God which remain to be revealed. In the course of this discussion Paul drives his argument back, in chapter 9, to the sovereign election of God as the foundation. His thinking proceeds along these lines:

Argument: It is not the existence and acceptance of Israel on which the promise of God depends,
But
The existence and acceptance of Israel *depend on the promise.*
This *promise* has always involved distinguishing among men:
a) Not all of Abraham's descendants were children of the promise (v. 7–8)
b) Not even having the same father guarantees grace (v. 10)
c) God's electing purpose is the great factor in grace (v. 11–13)

This, of course, is to put things so starkly that objections are almost inevitable, and Paul mentions and answers two of these:

Objection 1: Is God then unjust? (v. 14)
Answer: No, because we are not dealing here with justice but with mercy. Paul's point is that to ask for justice is really to ask for condemnation! Sinful man cannot plead before a holy God on the grounds of what he deserves. He can only cling to the mercy of God (v. 15 ff).

Objection 2: Does this not mean that God is arbitrary? (v. 19)
Answer: a) The man who speaks like this does not understand his sinful creatureliness before God (v. 20–21).
b) The man who speaks like this has not understood the purpose of God (v. 22 ff).

Naturally this outline needs to be developed and these verses studied with considerable care in order to feel the weight of Paul's argument. But what he is trying to say should already be clear. He is showing that the doctrine of God's electing purposes reveals his character. It shows the nature of grace as God's free and unfettered love and mercy for men. That light is so bright that it prods sinful man out of the last burrow of his own pride and self-sufficiency as he argues about his 'rights' and the necessity for 'justice'. How slow we are, even as Christians, really to believe that salvation is entirely by grace! We sing:

> *Not the labours of my hands*
> *Can fulfil Thy law's demands;*
> *Could my zeal no respite know,*
> *Could my tears for ever flow,*
> *All for sin could not atone:*
> *Thou must save, and Thou alone.*
>   Augustus Montague Toplady

What the doctrine of election expounded in Romans 9 is saying to us is: This is precisely the truth of the matter—your salvation depends entirely upon what God has done, in choosing you, sending his Son to die for you, and drawing you into his kingdom through the Holy Spirit!

(iii) Ephesians 1:4-14

Most scholars today are agreed that the letter to the Ephesians was originally a circular letter written to several churches in Asia Minor, one copy of which was intended specifically for Ephesus. That helps to explain the absence (in such an obviously warm letter) of personal greetings of any kind. It further contributes to our appreciation of the opening section of the letter in which Paul expresses his thanks for the salvation which is common to all believing people. He describes its preparation (1:4-5); its execution (1:6-7); its publication (1:8-10) and its application (1:11-14). Two things emerge very clearly. (i) To be a Christian is to be the recipient of great spiritual blessing and this redounds to the praise of God's grace (vv. 6, 7, 12, 14). (ii) All these blessings are found *in Christ* as we have previously noted, and are therefore rooted in God's *eternal* purposes (vv. 4, 5, 9, 11).

It is as though Paul were 'unpacking' for us the bundle of blessings which God has given us in his Son, and holding them up for us to see: Forgiveness, Redemption, Acceptance, and all we need to travel from this world to the next in the joy of the Lord. As he 'unpacks' these blessings it becomes clearer and clearer that he is speaking of a plan God has had before we were born. Even before the foundation of the world he began to pack all these blessings into Christ, and labelled them with my name!

These three passages constitute the most sustained of Paul's writings on this theme. But the doctrine pervades his letters (see for example, 1 Cor. 1:26-31; Eph. 2:10; Col. 1:27; 3:12; 2 Thess. 2:13; 2 Tim. 1:9). For Paul election was the best word of the gospel, because it was the first word of the gospel!

We have already seen, particularly in dealing with Romans 9-11, that this emphasis in Paul's teaching met with objections. We noted earlier too that it was partly this emphasis in Jesus' teaching which caused some to stop following him. As in those days, so today objections are brought against this teaching.

DIFFICULTIES ABOUT ELECTION AND PREDESTINATION

(i) Predestination denies free will

This is an age-old problem. If God chooses us, how freely, or even genuinely, do we choose God? In this connection three things should be said:

Firstly, if Scripture teaches us that God has chosen his believing people from all eternity, on that our hearts should rest, however mysterious it may seem to us to be. Until we have come to the place where we can sing about election with a full heart we have not grasped the spirit of the New Testament teaching.

Secondly, we do manage to reconcile God's will and our own will in personal religious experience. We know that we came to trust in Christ and exercised our own powers in doing so. *God did not believe for us! We* came to faith. Yet, at the same time we bow down before him to thank and praise him that he placed his hand upon us and brought us to himself. Indeed, when we pray for others, it is invariably in these terms: 'O Lord, come and draw him to yourself!' Someone taking a 'print-out' of what we believed from the evidence of our prayers might well come to the conclusion that we believed something strikingly similar to the teaching of the New Testament!

Thirdly, perhaps we should raise a question about our common belief in 'free will'. The phrase is only used by the Bible in the context of stewardship! It is never used in the context of coming to Christ in faith. It is also open to such a wide variety of interpretations that it has become almost meaningless in the context of any discussion on the purposes of God. In actual fact such biblical emphasis on man's will as there is, tends to emphasise its bondage rather than its freedom. Only as we increasingly appreciate the dark image of ourselves in the pages of the divine mirror of Scripture are we likely to yield up to God those final areas of our thinking where we have the innate tendency to smuggle into salvation some little contribution of our own.

(ii)   Predestination breeds pride and self-congratulation

Sometimes the biblical teaching has been misunderstood in this way. In the days of the Scots poet Robert Burns, in eighteenth-century Scotland, this doctrine was occasionally preached and understood without reference to its ethical and moral implications. The disastrous results Burns recorded in *Holy Willie's Prayer*—in words which can scarcely be read by a Christian without causing pain: Holy Willie is heard to pray thus:

> *O Thou that in the heavens does dwell*
> *Wha, as it pleases best Thysel,*
> *Sends ane to heaven and ten to h-ll,*
> *A' for Thy glory*
> *And no for any guid or ill*
> *They've done before Thee!*

The prayer goes on (as every Scottish child knows) to identify Willie as one of the 'elect', and then to catalogue a number of his vices—vices which in biblical teaching would disqualify him from any assurance that he had ever become a Christian at all. Willie's distorted understanding is that since he is one of the elect, all is well:

> *What was I, or my generation*
> *That I should get such exaltation?*

He is the epitome of self-congratulation.

This is a distortion of biblical teaching. We see the same distortion illustrated in Scripture. It was the great error of the Jews. But election truly understood promotes humility because it is the final confirmation to us that we contribute nothing to our salvation. So when election is rightly appreciated, poetry remains, but humility in it abounds:

> *'Tis not that I did choose Thee,*
> *For, Lord, that could not be;*
> *This heart would still refuse Thee*
> *Hadst Thou not chosen me.*
> *Thou from the sin that stained me*
> *Hast cleansed and set me free;*
> *Of old Thou hast ordained me,*
> *That I should live to Thee.*
>
> *'Twas sovereign mercy called me,*
> *And taught my opening mind;*
> *The world had else enthralled me,*
> *To heavenly glories blind,*
> *My heart owns none above Thee;*
> *For thy rich grace I thirst;*
> *This knowing, if I love Thee,*
> *Thou must have loved me first.*
>
> Josiah Conder

(iii) Predestination destroys moral effort

The conclusion is sometimes drawn, at least mentally, that if God has chosen us it is of no consequence how we live. But the New Testament lays great emphasis on the opposite! Election is the foundation of holiness. It is on the basis of the electing purposes of God which Paul had expounded in Romans 9–11 that he is able to make his appeal in Romans 12:1–2:

> Therefore, I urge you, brothers, in view of God's mercy, to offer your bodies as living sacrifices, holy and pleasing to God—which is your spiritual worship. Do not conform any longer to the pattern of this world, but be transformed by the renewing of your mind. Then you will be able to test and approve what God's will is—his good, pleasing and perfect will.

This theme runs consistently through the New Testament, as the following quotations indicate:

> For *he chose* us in him (Christ) before the creation of the world *to be holy and blameless in his sight.*
>
> Ephesians 1:4

> For *we are God's workmanship,* created in Christ Jesus *to do good works, which God prepared in advance* for us to do.
>
> Ephesians 2:10

> Therefore, *as God's chosen people,* holy and dearly loved, clothe yourselves with compassion, kindness, humility, gentleness and patience.
>
> Colossians 3:12

> We have been *chosen according to the foreknowledge of God the Father,* by the *sanctifying* work of the Spirit, *for obedience to Jesus Christ* and sprinkling by his blood.
>
> 1 Peter 1:2

The thrust of the biblical teaching is that election produces transformed living. It is the foundation of holiness, and consistently expresses itself in a life which is morally transformed through Spirit-filled obedience to the word of God. Nothing could be further from the truth than the suggestion that God's choice destroys moral effort on our part. On the contrary, it is a great and powerful encouragement to moral effort. If God has chosen us, what kind of lives should we live to his praise?

(iv) Predestination weakens evangelism

If God's sovereign choice of men is the foundation of their salvation, then there can be no point to preaching the gospel! Again the doctrine of election has sometimes been so misunderstood that this conclusion has been drawn—God's people in the Old Testament did not realise that they had been chosen for service and witness, to be a light to the Gentiles. Their *misunderstanding* of election destroyed a true evangelistic zeal. It may also be that in the Christian church some who have held this doctrine of election have failed in their evangelistic responsibilities. But that is an insecure argument, since men of entirely different persuasion likewise fail to evangelise. We ought not to employ two-edged arguments in such sensitive areas of discussion. Rather we should ask ourselves: If election and predestination are biblical doctrines *how* are these things related to evangelism?

It is a very helpful thing to study some New Testament passages with this question in mind. When we do so, we discover that the early church moved from thinking about election to thinking about evangelism in the most natural way possible. They undoubtedly learned this from our Lord's words in Matthew 11:25-8, already quoted, in which he turns from the mysteries of God's eternal purposes to a compassionate evangelistic appeal to the weak and heavy-laden. Similarly the apostle Paul moves from laying down the great principles of foreknowledge and predestination in Romans 8, to the application of these doctrines in particular to his evangelistic concern for the Jews in chapter 9, *via* one of the most moving sentences in all his writings:

> I speak the truth in Christ—I am not lying, my conscience confirms it in the Holy Spirit—I have great sorrow and unceasing anguish in my heart. For I could wish that I myself were cursed and cut off from Christ for the sake of my brothers, those of my own race, the people of Israel.
> Romans 9:1-4

> Brothers, my heart's desire and prayer to God for the Israelites is that they may be saved.
> Romans 10:1

It would then be more accurate to say that a proper understanding of God's electing purposes of grace led Paul to a strong evangelistic spirit. Moreover, this was the rock on which Paul found he needed to stand when faced with all kinds of discouraging opposition and at times apparent fruitlessness in his own ministry of the gospel. When the Corinthian Jews began to abuse him, and Paul found himself filled with alarm, the Lord spoke to him in a vision one night:

> Do not be afraid; keep on speaking, do not be silent. For I am with you, and no-one is going to attack and harm you, *because I have many people in this city.*
>
> Acts 18:9

The knowledge of electing grace was a solace and encouragement to him in such a dark and difficult period of his ministry.

Of course, this is not to answer all the questions which rise in our minds, or harmonise all the tensions we find in our thinking. But we have seen enough in the New Testament to realise that there election was not a dirge but a song of joy; not an obstacle to evangelism but an encouragement; not a promoter of pride but a producer of humility; not an influence to enervate moral effort but a summons to spare no energy to live a life pleasing and acceptable to God. Election, in the Scriptures, is something for which we worship God because in it he reveals the greatness and the freeness of his love for sinful men. At the end of the day we must confess that 'The secret things belong to the Lord our God, but the things revealed belong to us and our children for ever' (Deut. 29:29). But we must also confess:

> Praise be to the God and Father of our Lord Jesus Christ, who has blessed us in heavenly realms with every spiritual blessing in Christ. *For he chose us in him before the creation of the world . . .*

13
Sin's Dominion Ended

In the First Letter of John there is a very important insight into what is involved in becoming a Christian. In John's language this involves a birth from God. He takes up the picture of birth and develops it further when he tells us, 'No-one who is born of God will continue to sin, because God's seed remains in him; he cannot go on sinning, because he has been born of God' (1 Jn. 3:9). This is a very startling statement, particularly in some of the older translations which translate John's words, 'No-one born of God commits sin' (R.S.V.). But when we begin to feel the weight of John's teaching we come to recognise that what he is powerfully underlining is the fact that *in the new birth a radical alteration takes place in the life of the Christian in his relationship with sin.* He simply does not go on sinning. Indeed, from one point of view, he does not sin!

John's words are difficult to understand, and modern commentators list many possible interpretations of them. But the main drift of them is this: by the new birth a radical break with sin takes place. Although *the character of sin* in the Christian is no different from its character before he became a child of God, *the status of sin* has been dramatically changed. Exactly what this means and what its implications are will be discussed later in the present chapter. For the moment we will develop the thought which may already be present in your mind as you read: 'Surely the emphasis of the New Testament is on the importance of a prolonged struggle with sin in the Christian's life?'

Traditional teaching on the Christian life has rightly tended to emphasise that there are no short-cuts, no easy roads to success. But in every age there have been those who have suggested some special way, some new experience, formula, or teaching which brings more immediate results and lifts men on to a new plane of spiritual experience altogether. It was this kind of emphasis which made J. C. Ryle publish his classic popular study, *Holiness*. He wrote:

When people talk of having received 'such a blessing', and of having found 'the higher life', after hearing some earnest advocate of 'holiness by faith and self-consecration', while their families and friends see no improvement and no increased sanctity in their daily tempers and behaviour, immense harm is done to the cause of Christ. True holiness, we surely ought to remember, does not consist merely of inward sensations and impressions. It is much more than tears, and sighs, and bodily excitement, and a quickened pulse, and a passionate feeling of attachment to our own favourite preachers and our own religious party, and a readiness to quarrel with everyone who does not agree with us. It is something of 'the image of Christ', which can be seen and observed by others in our private life, and habits, and character, and doings.

Holiness, Introduction.

We cannot but agree with Ryle and deplore all instant methods of holy living. But, at the same time, it would be a distortion to present the New Testament teaching on sanctification *only* as a long, hard struggle for victory over sin as though few Christians (and those generally speaking of previous centuries!) ever lived the life of faith with any degree of success. In emphasising one danger we must not fall into another. For the fact of the matter is that the New Testament represents sanctification *as a process preceded and followed by two crises*. There is a crisis yet to come, in our glorification with Christ when we will be 'changed' (1 Cor. 15:51, 2). But there is also, according to the New Testament, a fundamental crisis which has already been experienced by the Christian, at the moment of his entry into the kingdom of God. If there is any 'secret' to understanding the doctrine of sanctification and to living a life of holiness, then this is it. Several considerations in the teaching of Paul give rise to this view.

(i) In the New Testament, every Christian is a 'saint', a 'holy one'. This does not express the idea of a progressive development towards a condition of holiness, but rather suggests a presently enjoyed status of holiness.

(ii) Certain key passages of the New Testament can only be understood if sanctification is thought of as a past experience. In 1 Corinthians 6:11, Paul speaks of the believers in these terms: 'But you were washed, you were sanctified, you were justified in the name of the Lord Jesus Christ and by the Spirit of our God.' The verbs are in the past tense and the normal order of things has been reversed. We would ordinarily have anticipated Paul would have written 'justified, sanctified'. Why then reverse the order? The order reflects a profound truth in Paul's theology. There is a sense in which sanctification not only follows justification, but precedes it. There is a rather similar use in Acts 20:32, where Paul speaks of 'all those who are sanctified'. Peter has a similar striking reversal of anticipated order in his First Letter, when he writes: 'we have been chosen according to the foreknowledge of God the Father, by the sanctifying work of the Spirit, for obedience to Jesus Christ and sprinkling by his blood' (1 Pet. 1:2). Surely obedience to Christ should precede sanctification by the Spirit? Normally, yes; but here again Peter is alluding to a critical sanctification which takes place at the very outset of Christian experience.

This germinal thought is worked out very fully by Paul when he begins to explore the significance of the Christian's union with Christ in terms of our relationship with sin.

Often when union with Christ in his death is spoken of in the New Testament, it is with special reference to the significance of his death for his and our relationship to sin. This is true of passages like Colossians 2:20–3:14, Galatians 2:20, and particularly of Romans 6:1–14 which we will look at in some detail. It provides us with the most explicit and detailed description of the new status which the Christian has in relationship to sin.

Dying to Sin

> What shall we say, then? Shall we go on sinning, so that grace may increase? By no means! We died to sin; how can we live in it any longer?
>
> Romans 6:1–2

Paul's main theme to this point in Romans has been justification. He is vindicating his teaching against the accusation that it encourages carelessness in Christian living because it is a doctrine of the justification of the ungodly. Paul had gone so far in magnifying the grace of God in Christ in Romans 5:20 that he had stated that where sin abounded (in Adam and then throughout mankind) grace had super-abounded (in Christ and now in us). But, it was objected to this teaching: If this is so, then the more we sin the more grace God will reveal; therefore, we can sin to our heart's content and promote the grace of God rather than incur his wrath.

Paul answers this in the powerful passage which follows. He reacts with every fibre of his being to the suggestion because it is a distortion of the truth. He argues that the grace which justifies us is the grace which also sanctifies us. In particular, the grace which brings us into fellowship with Christ for justification is the grace which unites us to Christ in such a way that we have 'died to sin' (v. 12). If we have died to sin we cannot go on living in it!

The heart of the argument is expressed in these words: 'We died to sin.' Our translations are scarcely able to bring out Paul's precise nuance of meaning, for the relative pronoun he uses conveys the idea 'we *who are the kind of people who* have . . .' It stresses a major characteristic of the subject. When in English we express a strong sense of disappointment with someone by saying: 'How could *you, you* of all people; *you*, the last person I would have expected to do such a thing—how could *you* . . .?' we are employing the same kind of language. It is an expression which reaches down to the basic inconsistency between what the person is in terms of his status and relationships, and what he has done. The Christian, by virtue of his being a Christian, cannot continue in sin. To do so contradicts what he is. It is the same point as John's: we do not go on sinning because of who we are, namely, those in whom the divine seed resides. Here, in Romans 6, the point is this: we do not continue in sin for the simple reason that *we are the kind of people who have died to sin.*

The same emphasis is brought out more fully by Paul in a later verse when he speaks of those who 'have been united with him (Christ) in his death' (Rom. 6:5). The word he uses here means literally 'to be born with', 'innate', 'congenital'. It implies that the death of Christ is something which was part of our Christian lives from our spiritual rebirth. Since it was, in Christ's case, a 'death to sin', so it must also be in ours. Ever since the day when by God's mighty power we were born from above we have had this radically new relationship to sin. The tragedy is that so many of us either do not know it or do not live in the light of it.

Paul's Argument

At this stage it is extremely important that we follow through the teaching Paul expounds in Romans 6 that the believer has 'died to sin'. This is a great and liberating truth. That is why over the years a whole literature has accumulated around it. I remember in my teens being thrilled by some of the biographical accounts and illustrations I read of it. But often, at the end of the day, the whole wonder of it drifted into the mists because these shared experiences and illustrations were not based on a painstaking exposition of Scripture, so that I was left with no solid ground on which to plant my own feet and to build my own experience. Hard work though it may seem, the primary need we all have is to try to master Paul's *exposition* of this truth in the sure confidence that in this way the truth will soon master our hearts too.

The heart of what Paul says is that in Christ the Christian has died to sin and is raised to a new life to God. In the verses which follow the apostle works this out in three stages.

(i) Our death to sin is accomplished through union with Christ.

> Or don't you know that all of us who were baptised into Christ Jesus were baptised into his death? We were therefore buried with him through baptism into death in order that, just as Christ was raised from the dead through the glory of the Father, we too may live a new life.
> If we have been united with him in his death, we will certainly also be united with him in his resurrection.
> Romans 6:3–5

Paul's appeal is to the significance of their *baptism*. They were baptised into Christ (v. 3—whether in the reality of Spirit-baptism, or the symbol of water baptism, the point remains the same). But if they were baptised into Christ, it was into a Christ who died and rose, so that they have been baptised into his death and resurrection. Just as Christ's death led him to a new, resurrection life to God, the same is true of the Christian who has been united to him.

Point 1 in the argument therefore is this: Those who have died and been raised with Christ to newness of life cannot consistently live in sin. To do so would be a denial of their new identity (we are the kind of men who have died to sin!).

(ii) Our union with Christ involves the death of 'the old man'.

> For we know that our old self was crucified with him so that the body of sin might be rendered powerless, that we should no longer be slaves to sin—because anyone who has died is freed from sin.
>
> Romans 6:6–7

Here Paul appeals to what the Roman Christians already know. Would that all the Lord's people were Roman Christians! The main lines of what he says are not difficult to follow through and we can state the argument before going on to examine it in greater detail.

Point 2 in the argument is: If we are freed from sin we cannot go on living as though we were still under its dominion.

But the way in which this is demonstrated and the precise point Paul is here making require further investigation. For one thing, Paul employs several unusual expressions and then goes on to tell us that we have been 'freed' from sin. His words cry out for explanation!

The *'old man'* is what we were before we were united to Christ, 'the man we once were' as the New English Bible renders it. More than that, Paul perhaps means the man we were in Adam. He had already expounded this in the previous section of Romans (5:12–21). When we came to Christ, and were made one with him, that 'old man' was crucified with Christ and died.

The *'body of sin'* is best explained as the body in which we live seen as the vehicle which sin employs as its slave, the body characterised by sin's dominion. This 'body of sin' is 'rendered powerless', or 'destroyed' (A.V., R.S.V.). Paul is not saying that indwelling sin is destroyed but rather that its status and dominion have been broken in our lives through Christ. Formerly it reigned like a king (cf. 5:21) but now, although still present it has been de-throned and no longer has a rightful claim upon our lives. On the basis of this Paul is later able to exhort us: 'Therefore do not let sin reign in your mortal body so that you obey its evil desires' (6:12).

The *crucifixion of the old man* and the *destruction of the body of sin* make an enormous difference to our lives. We are no longer what we once were; we are no longer related to sin the way we once were. It is this new relationship which we must examine a little more carefully. The consequence of the crucifixion of the old man and the rendering powerless of the body of sin is *that we should no longer be slaves to sin*. The reason given for this is in the form of a self-evident principle: *anyone who has died has been freed from sin*. The great question of course is: What does it mean to be 'freed from sin'?

Clearly there are certain things it cannot mean. Paul cannot by any stretch of the imagination be suggesting that the Christian ceases his struggle with sin. He is not speaking about a certain class of Christians who have 'come to victory' (as such an interpretation usually assumes). He is speaking of something which is universally true of believers. Nor can he mean that the Christian ceases sinning altogether, for as his argument progresses we see that this freedom from sin is the basis for our struggle against sin:

> *Therefore*, do not let sin reign ... Do not offer the parts of your body to sin.

It has frequently been held that Paul's language suggests that the Christian is 'justified from sin'. The very word Paul uses *is* the verb 'to be justified'. This interpretation warrants examination. Those who have adopted this position have tended to do so in opposition to any suggestion that the Christian is sinless, immune to temptation, or rid of indwelling sin. In that opposition I think they are right. But there are reasons for believing that Paul means *more* than that Christians are 'declared righteous' in connection with sin:

The words appear in a context of sanctification, not one of justification. Further, Paul is speaking about the slavery of sin, and salvation in that context must mean more than justification.

Then, again, later in the passage Paul actually says we are 'freed' from sin, using the ordinary verb for setting free (*eleutheroō*) in verses 18 and 22. That would suggest that he uses the word 'justify' here in the sense of the former relationship with sin being ended.

What then does Paul mean by saying that we are no longer *enslaved* to sin because we have been 'set free' from it? Two things help to clarify the answer. In the first place in Romans 5:12–6:23, Paul is thinking of sin as a master, a tyrant which enslaves us. That is why in the original Greek text he constantly uses the expression *'The Sin'*, personifying its power as he speaks of its reign in the lives of men and of their slavery and thraldom to it. Secondly, Paul actually uses the language of slavery to describe the former relationship to sin which was ours. These considerations suggest that what he is speaking about is the rule, dominion or reign of sin in the life of the believer. That rule has been broken and abolished in Christ, Sin no longer has the same authority *even although its nature is unchanged*. It is from such a perspective that a life of settled victory over present indwelling sin is a possibility.

(iii)   Our union with Christ leads to new life in him.

> Now if we died with Christ, we believe that we will also live with him. For we know that since Christ was raised from the dead, he cannot die again; death no longer has mastery over him. The death he died, he died to sin once for all; but the life he lives, he lives to God.
>
> Romans 6:8–10

Paul takes his argument one stage further. We are united to Christ, and therefore united to him in his death. But Christ's death and resurrection are inseparable. We therefore can be assured of this, that, united to a Christ who died once to sin (coming himself under its dominion in order that he might die for our guilt), we are also united to the Christ who was raised and now in newness of life lives for ever to God. What was true of Christ is also true of us. We not only have a new relationship with sin, but share in his new life!

Point 3 in the argument therefore is: We do not continue in sin, not only because we have died to it, but also because, by our very nature as Christians, we are living new lives to the glory of God.

Practical Implications

And so the apostle brings us to his application. If all this is true, it should have the most practical implications. Sin does not have dominion over us! Since that is the case, we are to make sure, by fighting against its every movement, that it does not invade our hearts *as though it had dominion*. If we consider ourselves to be what we truly are, he argues, dead men brought to life in Christ; if we build on this sure foundation, refusing to yield our body to sin as its slave, then we will discover that the *assurance* Paul gives us, 'sin shall not be your master' will also be our daily *experience*.

What practical difference does this really make to Christian living?

Perhaps a simple illustration will help to reinforce the significance of this teaching. When I was a little boy there was a children's record request programme on B.B.C. Radio. One of the songs, regularly played towards the end of the programme because of its popularity, was called 'The Ugly Duckling' sung by Danny Kaye. It told the story of a rather self-conscious little 'duckling', mixing with the other birds and feeling very sorry for himself because of his 'feathers all stubby and brown'. He was rather despised by his fellow birds, and felt something of a failure, especially when he cast a side-long glance at their comparative beauty. Then one day the 'ugly duckling' looked down, and saw something marvellous. He no longer had brown, ugly feathers, but was arrayed in the splendid white feathers of a swan! And off he went shouting, 'I'm a swan, I'm a swan'. Although he had thought he was a duckling, he had never been a duckling. He had been a swan all the time. But the real difference came when he saw what he really was. The recognition of his true identity was the beginning of new joy!

Precisely the same is true of the teaching of this chapter. The great mistake many of us make is to look *only* at our sin and failure, and then ask, a little despairingly, What can I do? But our need is not *to do*, it is first of all *to understand what God has done*. To see that what he has made us through his Son is a man or a woman who has died with Christ to sin's dominion and has been raised with Christ to newness of life. We are those over whom sin has no longer any dominion. Like the 'ugly duckling' then, I may say: 'I'm not under sin's dominion! I am a new creature! I am not what I thought I was, nor what I once was! I'm not an "ugly duckling" Christian, I'm a child of God!'

> We who are the kind of people who have died with Christ to sin.
> We who are the kind of people who have been raised with Christ to life.
> *How can we, of all people, continue to live as though sin reigned?*

> *And shall we then go on to sin,*
> *that grace may more abound?*
> *Great God, forbid that such a thought*
> *should in our breast be found!*

> *With Christ the Lord we dy'd to sin;*
> *with him to life we rise,*
> *To life, which now begun on earth,*
> *is perfect in the skies.*

> *Too long enthrall'd to Satan's sway,*
> *we now are slaves no more;*
> *For Christ hath vanquish'd death and sin,*
> *our freedom to restore.*

But this freedom from the dominion of sin is not the end of our struggle against sin. In fact it is the beginning of a new conflict with it. For while we have died to sin, sin has not died in us. We must now therefore examine this new conflict more closely.

14
The Christian's Conflicts

We are always trying to tie down the doctrine of the Christian life to our own satisfaction. But the harmony of true Christian living cannot be sustained by an emphasis on only one aspect of Christian experience. It is possible to move among Christians who regard anything but a tranquil freedom from the ravages of sin as an indication of little faith. On the other hand there are those whose view of the Christian pilgrimage is so gloomy that one might almost be forgiven for thinking they believed the only salvation worth having lay somewhere in the future. But being a Christian is not meant to be a rather miserable prelude to a future bliss which is not quite sufficiently certain enough to shed a ray of light upon the present!

It would be a sad and mistaken thing to adopt either of these extreme positions. The Christian life is not all smiles; but neither is it all tears. It is not all peace, but neither is it only unabated defeat. There is 'all joy and peace in believing' (Rom. 15:13 R.S.V.) but yet at the same time the Christian life involves what the *Westminster Confession* called 'a continual and irreconcilable war'.

The New Testament sees the coming of Christ (including his incarnation, life, death, resurrection and ascension) as intersecting time and in a dramatic way altering its flow and filling all present time with special significance. The person who is a Christian lives at a unique period of human history, between the first coming of Christ which inaugurated what the Bible calls 'the last days', and the return of Christ, which will usher in the end of the world. The Christian's life therefore bears all the marks of this interim period in which the fruit of Christ's work and victory begins to be seen in the world and in the lives of individuals as well as corporately in the new society of the church. We are already 'saved' by grace (Eph. 2:8), but there is a sense in which we are 'being saved' through Christ's work within us, and a further sense in which we will not be fully saved until Christ returns and we are transformed into his image. We live 'between the times'.

Oscar Cullmann, the Continental New Testament theologian, has popularised a vivid illustration from the events of the Second World War in this context. In biblical teaching, the Cross and its attendant events is D-Day, when the decisive conflict has been engaged and won, V-Day is the day to which we look forward when what was settled on D-Day will become a totally fulfilled reality. The Christian possesses the assurance of victory over all his enemies, but none the less faces a situation in which minor skirmishes and mopping-up operations are an integral part of life. In terms of the teaching we considered in the previous chapter, the Christian has died to sin in Christ's dying victory, but sin itself has not yet been destroyed. It remains sin still, and as we will see in the next chapter must be dealt with as sin. The vital truth enshrined in Paul's teaching is that we have a quite different relationship to sin now that we have entered into the victory of D-Day. But until we arrive at the ultimate destruction of sin on V-Day, we will inevitably be engaged in warfare against it and will find ourselves faced with constant conflicts. It never ceases to be true of the Christian that he approaches Christ with *'fightings and fears within, without'*. To some aspects of the nature of this 'irreconcilable war' we must now turn. They come from two sources, as Charlotte Elliott (following Paul, 2 Cor. 7:5) shrewdly noticed—'without' and 'within'.

The New Testament suggests that the sources of temptation and therefore the primary areas of conflict in Christian experience are three-fold: *the world, the flesh* and *the devil*. These are the powers that hold sway apart from Jesus Christ. Before the Ephesians became Christians they were like the rest of mankind, dominated by 'the ways of this world' and by 'the ruler of the kingdom of the air, the spirit who is now at work in those who are disobedient', and were found 'gratifying the cravings of our sinful nature and following its desires and thoughts' (Eph. 2:2-3). It is the classical three-fold cord which is never easily broken—the world, the flesh and the devil which reappears in the first letter of John:

> I write to you young men, because you are strong, and the word of God lives in you, and you have overcome the evil one. Do not love the world or anything in the world. If

anyone loves the world, the love of the Father is not in him. For everything in the world—the cravings of sinful man, the lust of his eyes and the boasting of what he has and does—comes not from the Father but from the world.

1 John 2:14–17

The conflict 'without' is with the world and the devil; the conflict 'within' is with the flesh.

THE WORLD

The apostle Paul had a very significant way of greeting his fellow Christians. The Corinthians were '*in Corinth* ... sanctified *in Christ Jesus*' (1 Cor. 1:2). The Ephesians were 'saints *in Ephesus*, the faithful *in Christ Jesus*' (Eph. 1:1). The Philippians were '*in Christ* Jesus *at Philippi*' (Phil. 1:1). His words graphically join together the two directions in which the Christian's life is drawn. The ultimate truth about him is that he is 'in Christ'. Christ is his home, and he belongs to him. He is living in the light of D-Day and the anticipation of V-Day. But he is also at Ephesus, or Corinth or Philippi where there are temptations, forces and general trends which are inimical to faithfulness to Jesus Christ. The calling of the Christian is to live a life that is consistent with his fellowship with Jesus in a world that is out of fellowship with Jesus. We are 'in Christ', but we are also in London, or Glasgow, or Manchester, or New York, or Hong Kong, or Melbourne. We love and serve Jesus and keep close to him, but we ride to work each day past the enticing adverts; we take the escalator from the 'tube' below to the fresh air above, remembering the promises Christ gave us earlier in the day in his word. But from both sides of us beckon the many temporal pleasures of the flesh deliberately packaged to capture us precisely at our weakest points and to overcome us when resistance is low. You and I are 'in Christ', but we are also 'in the world'. Of course our comfort is this—Christ wills us to be here. Has he not prayed for us:

> My prayer is not that you take them out of the world but that you protect them from the evil one. They are not of the world, even as I am not of it. Sanctify them by thy truth.
>
> John 17:15–17

But there is a sense in which this increases rather than lessens the tension, heightens rather than alleviates the battle. We face a consistent onslaught from outside of ourselves. The world is a very real source of temptation. It 'squeezes us into its mould', and often we are hard put to resist the pressure of its influence. The New Testament indicates a variety of ways in which the world makes its impression on men. In the parable of the Sower and the soils, Jesus describes the response to the word of God of the 'thorny heart':

> As for what was sown among thorns, this is he who hears the word, but the cares of the world and the delight in riches choke the word and it proves unfruitful.
> Matthew 13:22 (R.S.V.)

Here the world order is pictured as *choking* the grace of God in his word. Jesus is speaking about the way in which a professing disciple may allow devotion to possessions (whether he has them or lacks them!) to exist side by side with devotion to God. Eventually (for the process is slow, often unnoticed, but inexorable) the breath is sucked out of the voice of God's word in our hearts—and any spiritual vitality we formerly knew dies. The 'world', in the sense of the present age and all that belongs to it, with its values and time-bound perspectives must never be allowed to be a dominant factor in this way. That means, inevitably, that as Christians we must be constantly battling against the disorders of our own affections.

Paul sheds an illuminating sidelight on this same area in his often misunderstood words in 1 Corinthians 7:

> I would like you to be free from concern. An unmarried man is concerned about the Lord's affairs—how he can please the Lord. But a married man is concerned about the affairs of this world—how he can please his wife—and his interests are divided. An unmarried woman or virgin is concerned about the Lord's affairs: Her aim is to be devoted to the Lord in both body and spirit. But a married woman is concerned about the affairs of this world—how she can please her husband. I am saying this for your own good, not to restrict you, but that you may live in a right way in undivided devotion to the Lord.
> 1 Corinthians 7:32-5

On occasion these words have been taken to reflect a very low view of marriage on Paul's part. But men who have lived through revival days like the ones the church at Corinth was undoubtedly experiencing, and who have been sensitive to their Christian responsibilities, have often come to realise that Paul was advocating realism rather than masochism. He was not thinking about marriage as a battle-ground, but of the inward battles the married person would have to fight with himself or herself to maintain a spirit of loyal devotion to Jesus Christ. Marriage is a blessing (as Paul clearly indicates in his letters to Colosse and Ephesus). That is why it can also be a source of temptation. It is the paradox of earthly blessing that because of our own wayward hearts we can worship the gift rather than the giver. So, earlier on in the same chapter, Paul speaks about cultivating a spirit of detachment from the world:

> What I mean, brothers, is that the time is short. From now on those who have wives should live as if they had none: those who mourn, as if they did not; those who are happy as if they were not; those who buy something as if it were not theirs to keep; those who use the things of the world, as if not engrossed in them. For this world in its present form is passing away.
> 1 Corinthians 7:29–31

Calvin's remarks are outstandingly helpful here:

> All the things which make for the enriching of this present life are sacred gifts of God, but we spoil them by our misuse of them. If we want to know the reason why, it is because we are always entertaining the delusion that we will go on for ever in this world. The result is that the very things which ought to be of assistance to us in our pilgrimage through life, become chains which bind us. In order to shake us out of our stupor the apostle quite rightly calls us back to think about the shortness of life. From this he infers that the way in which we ought to make use of all the things of this world, is, as if we do not possess them. For the man who thinks of himself as an alien sojourner in the world, uses the things of the world as if they belonged to someone else; in other words, as things which are lent for

the day only. The point is that the mind of a Christian ought not to be filled with thoughts of earthly things, or find satisfaction in them, for we ought to be living as if we might have to leave this world at any moment ... the apostle is not advising Christians, here, to get rid of their possessions. All that he asks for is that they do not find them completely engrossing.

First Corinthians, pp. 159–60

The world *moulds* us, as well as *chokes* us, says Paul. We have to make every effort to avoid the danger of its grip pressurising us into conformity with its way of thinking. Worldliness, in this sense, is not to be reduced to fast cars and bright lights. It is a much deeper and more sinister thing altogether—the invasion of our whole perception of reality by a set of standards which are sub-biblical and sub-Christian. A man can be outwardly conformed to the Christian way of life while he is inwardly conformed to the spirit of this world. That was the great fault of some of the Pharisees. They were 'other-worldly' in the most 'this-worldly' way imaginable. This is an exceedingly subtle danger, an almost invincible task-master, and a highly elusive characteristic when we try to detect it in ourselves. But it is one of the curses which besets evangelical Christianity. It is seen every time we observe the traditions of the fathers but do so in the lifeless spirit which has been created by love of the present age.

The snare of the world is that *it draws us from Christ*. We do not know precisely what the cause of Demas' desertion from Paul was. Did he apostatise as well as quit the apostolic band? We cannot say. But we do know what caused his separation from Paul. Instead of living as one who loved the appearing of Christ (2 Tim. 4:8), 'he loved this world' (2 Tim. 4:10). Something in this present age, in this world order, drew him away from his first love for Christ and for his suffering people. Demas must, at least momentarily, have seen what was happening to him. But perhaps by that time it was too late! He had lost so much spiritual power that apparently he found no assurance in the truth which the apostle John was to state:

> everyone born of God has overcome the world. This is the victory that has overcome the world, even our faith. Who is

it that overcomes the world? Only he who believes that Jesus is the Son of God.

1 John 5:4–5

The Devil

The world, however, is inanimate. The Christian faces another dimension of conflict with an animate enemy. He engages in conflict with Satan. When we think about the conflict with Satan there are twin dangers to be avoided. The first is that of paying too little attention to him. The second is the error of making too much of him so that we lose sight of Christ and his victory, or are paralysed with irrational fears about the power of evil, or even begin to live as though, with diminished responsibility, we were the helpless pawns of his strategies. None of these attitudes corresponds to the realism and the sense of victory which pervades the New Testament teaching. There the full force of Satan's power is recognised, but it is looked upon in the light of Christ's victory. Indeed, it is axiomatic in our understanding of Christian doctrine that it is only in the light of the full revelation of God in Christ that we can perceive the kingdom of darkness clearly enough to understand its powers. In the Old Testament Satan is a relatively shadowy figure, just as in the same pages Christ appears only between the lines. But when we turn the pages of the New Testament we discover that Christ's coming drew Satan out of the shadows, and in many passages he appears fully revealed as the instigator of sin and sorrow. Several features of this New Testament unveiling should be noticed:

(i) The person and work of Satan

The Bible's position is that Satan is a creature, made by God for his own glory. Many Christians have seen hints of his origin and fall in such Old Testament passages as Isaiah 14:12–17 and Ezekiel 28:11–19. But by no means is that interpretation universally held. John Calvin, for example (who could scarcely be accused of not believing in the personal existence of Satan) wrote about the former passage:

> The exposition of this passage which some have given, as if it referred to Satan, has arisen from ignorance, for the con-

text shows that these statements must be understood in reference to the King of the Babylonians.

Isaiah, I, p. 442

None the less, there are clear statements in the New Testament which would seem to be best understood as allusions to Satan's fall. Jesus speaks of Satan as 'a murderer from the beginning, *not holding to the truth*, for there is no truth in him' (Jn. 8:44). John adds in his First Letter that 'the devil has been sinning *from the beginning*' (1 Jn. 3:8). Some unimaginable rebellion appears to have taken place in the kingdom of heaven before the Fall of man. More than that we probably cannot say. More than that we do not require to know.

What we can learn from with profit, however, is the list of names by which Satan is designated in the New Testament. Just as the titles for Christ tell us much about him, so the titles used for Satan tell us more than that he is a liar (Jn. 8:44) and a hinderer (1 Thess. 2:18).

He is the *Devil*. The name comes from the Greek verb *to throw*, and came to mean throwing in the sense of slandering. As is his name, so is his nature. The Devil trades in false statements. He twists the truth about Christ, and about the character of God in the world at large (how few people have any clear idea of the depths of God's love for men and its holy nature!), but also in the hearts of Christians. How insidiously he infers in the conscience of God's children that their Saviour is 'not really' all that he is made out to be. It is better, wiser, safer, suggests the Devil, not to trust Christ too far.

He is also called *Satan*. Some scholars have suggested that the root idea of this word conveys the sense of someone lying in ambush. If that is so it graphically portrays a common element of Christian conflict. For we often are not aware how or why times of temptation, stress, conflict and evil pressure have appeared. There can be no doubt that some of the irrational fears, doubts and thoughts which Christians experience should be traced back to the ambush in which Satan hides.

He is also called the *Deceiver*. In Revelation 13:11 we read about 'another beast, coming out of the earth. He had two horns like a lamb, but he spoke like a dragon.' In Revelation the lamb-figure normally represents Christ. It is no accident that this demonic beast bears some of Christ's outward characteristics, for it is the purpose of our enemy to deceive us and lead us astray. In fact the word used for 'deceive' basically means 'to cause to wander or stray' and so, 'to lead into error, or to deceive'. What an accurate picture, and one which is so consistent with everything else we know about the Devil! Right at the very start of human history the Bible tells us he employed deceit to captivate Eve, and Paul explicitly states this: 'the woman who was *deceived*' (1 Tim. 2:14). He blinds the minds of men and so is able to lead them astray (2 Cor. 4:4).

He is called the *Accuser of the brethren*. The word is *katēgoros*. It comes from a verb which means 'to accuse before a tribunal'. It is the picture of the Devil as the counsel for the prosecution against the child of God, bringing before the court the sins and misdeeds of the believer's life, demanding that he be cut off from the presence of God. The Devil is one who makes believers' guilt and failures his stock in trade.

> *Bowed down beneath a load of sin*
> *By Satan sorely pressed,*
> *By war without and fears within,*
> *I come to Thee for rest.*
>
> *Be Thou my Shield and Hiding-place*
> *That, sheltered near Thy side,*
> *I may my fierce accuser face,*
> *And tell him Thou hast died.*
>
> John Newton

(ii) Distinguishing Christ from Satan

The apostle Paul assures us that we not only know something of the person of Satan, but also that 'we are not unaware of his schemes' (2 Cor. 2:11). We have noted that one of these schemes is to distort our perception of his presence. He appears masquerading as an angel of light (2 Cor. 11:14). This raises for us a most pressing practical question. How can we distinguish the voice of Satan, and his hand in our affairs, from the voice and hand of our Lord Jesus Christ? How, by an appreciation of the difference, can we guard ourselves against Satan's wiles, and employ the 'whole armour of God'? There are four ways in which we can distinguish the true leading of Christ from the deceptive work of the Devil:

(a) *Christ's voice is always in accord with the true meaning and application of Scripture*, while Satan often mishandles Scripture and employs it for ends other than those for which it was originally given.

(b) *Christ's wisdom has the characteristics of Christ himself. It is pure and peace-loving* (Jas. 3:17). But by contrast it is often characteristic of the work of Satan that he brings and breeds restlessness and discontent. The 'wisdom' he sows himself, or through his agents, brings disagreement and mars the harmony between our own hearts and God's, and also between our own lives and those of our fellow-Christians.

(c) *Christ's entreaties are gentle, just as he himself is gentle.* But the entreaties of Satan are described by Paul as 'flaming arrows' (Eph. 6:16). They set the mind on fire, producing panic in the will, unbalancing our faith.

(d) *Christ calls us into the fellowship of his suffering* (Phil. 3:10), but the great hall-mark of Satan's leading is to draw us away from that union and fellowship with Christ and his Cross. Just as he endeavoured to draw the Lord Christ away from the Cross, first in the wilderness temptations and later through Simon Peter (Mk. 8:33), so he wants to take our affections as far away as possible from loving and trusting our suffering and crucified Master. He knows that the principle of the Cross is the seed-bed of spiritual usefulness (Jn. 12:24-26). He will pay any price to prevent us from practical experience of it.

But even when we have learned that mature spiritual discernment which enables us to distinguish between Christ and a disguised Satan like this, we have one further area to guard.

(iii) Distinguishing between Satan and our own hearts

In some ways this is a yet more difficult task, for the fundamental reason that there is a kinship between the remnants of indwelling sin in our hearts and the designs of the Evil One. We look in vain, by and large, for spiritual guidance at this kind of level in today's church. But once more we can be helped by the communion of saints. Thomas Watson, the rector of St Stephen's Walbrook in London in the middle of the seventeenth century wrote on this precise question:

How shall we perceive when a motion comes from our own hearts, and when from Satan?

It is hard, as Bernard says, to distinguish *inter morsum serpentis et morbum mentis* [between the bite of the serpent and the disease of the mind], between those suggestions which come from Satan, and which breed out of our own hearts. But I conceive there is this three-fold difference:

1. Such motions to evil as come from our own hearts spring up more leisurely, and by degrees. Sin is long concocted in the thoughts, ere consent be given; but usually we may know a motion comes from Satan by its suddenness. Temptation is compared to a dart, because it is shot suddenly. Eph. 6:16. David's numbering the people was a motion which the devil injected suddenly.

2. The motions to evil which come from our own hearts are not so terrible. Few are frightened at the sight of their own children; but motions coming from Satan are more ghastly and frightful, as motions to blasphemy and self-murder. Hence it is that temptations are compared to fiery darts, because, as flashes of fire, they startle and affright the soul. Eph. 6:16.

3. When evil thoughts are thrown into the mind, when we loathe and have reluctance to them; when we strive against them, and flee from them, as Moses did from the serpent, it shows they are not the natural birth of our own heart, but the hand of Joab is in this. 2 Sam. 14:19. Satan has injected these impure emotions.

A Body of Divinity, p. 588

Clearly there is no easy way. At no point of our experience do we come to the place where we can rely on a fool-proof system which will lead us unharmed through our pilgrimage. We follow a Shepherd, and we must always have our gaze fixed towards him. As we grow in grace and in the knowledge of God's word and his ways, we will naturally become more sensitive to the distinctions between the imaginations of our own minds, the temptations of our own hearts, the workings of Satan, and the clear voice of Christ. To recognise his voice is the privilege of every Christian (Jn. 10:27). It is a voice which becomes more distinguishable as we obey it. But the more we obey it, the more determination will Satan show in his efforts to confuse us and lead us astray. Surely to be a Christian is to be engaged in an 'irreconcilable war'! In the next chapter we will have to consider how the battles which it involves take place not only with an enemy outside of our lives, but also with a fifth column of resistance within our own hearts.

15
Crucifying Sin

In the previous chapter we began to consider the various conflicts in which the Christian is engaged, and in doing so concentrated on what we called the conflicts 'without'. That is not to say, of course, that these spiritual battles are fought 'over our heads' as it were. The enemies we face attack us from outside our own hearts and move inward with insistent force to draw our affections towards themselves and away from our Lord Jesus Christ. But their power rests on a further factor, namely the 'landing ground' they are able to find within our own lives.

When our Lord detected that his hour had come and that Satan was now advancing to meet him, he was able to say that 'he has no hold on me' (Jn. 14:30). There was nothing in our Lord's character which could be employed as a natural fulcrum by which Satan could lever his way into Jesus' life. But, sadly, that is not true of us. We have already hinted that there is still, in the Christian, a base of operations from which Satan is able to work, an enemy within, a 'Quisling' of the heart. We are faced with the prospect of recognising and dealing with this problem.

The cause of our battle 'within' is the continuing presence of indwelling sin. When we discussed Paul's teaching that the Christian has died to sin, we noted that this does not mean that sin has died in him. It remains, and it is still sin. What has changed is not its presence within our hearts, but its status (it no longer reigns) and our relationship to it (we are no longer its slaves). We saw what a radical thing this is and what a glorious deliverance it provides. But it does so in order that we may deal with sin in our Christian life from a perspective of victory. Not only has our relationship to it changed, but God has planted within us his divine seed (1 Jn. 3:9), and in this sense has 'added' to our powers as well as subtracting from sin's status! We have good reason to enter the conflict with the enemy of sin in optimistic mood! Not for a moment, however, dare we delude ourselves into thinking that the victory will be won consistently without blood, sweat and tears. *Surviving sin*, let it be said once more, *is not reigning sin, but it is real sin.*

This picture is further elucidated in the New Testament. The conflict within is heightened by the tension between 'the flesh' and 'the Spirit'. Here 'the flesh' does not mean 'the body'. It means *the whole man* in his creatureliness, weakness and sinfulness. Consequently among the sins of the flesh Scripture lists activities of the mind as well as of the body (cf. Gal. 5:19–21). 'The flesh in this sense,' writes Dr Leon Morris, 'denotes the whole personality of man as organised in the wrong direction, as directed to earthly pursuits rather than the service of God' (*New Bible Dictionary*, p. 426). In a word it is human nature dominated by sin.

But the Christian is not 'in the flesh' (Rom. 8:9 R.S.V). He is 'in the Spirit'. He is dominated by Christ through the Spirit. Yet the flesh remains in him in the sense that sin remains in him. Two further considerations must be mentioned. (i) While the flesh remains, the Spirit of God, operating *via* the new life God has given us, makes war on the flesh (Gal. 5:17). As new creatures we would battle against it in any case but this is an added encouragement. (ii) Paul tells us that 'those who belong to Christ have crucified the flesh with its passions and desires' (Gal. 5:24). These words need to be clearly distinguished from the teaching of such passages as Romans 6:1 ff and Galatians 2:20. Here Paul does not describe the decisive act of God in us through union with Christ, but *our* decisive rejection of sin when we join ourselves to Christ by faith. The language is harsh, but realistic. It refers to the brutal (and unnatural) response which the believer decisively made to sin at his conversion, and which he ratifies throughout the whole course of his Christian life.

Perhaps we can best summarise the situation in a table format:

For God	*Against God*
The new creature	The flesh
The Holy Spirit	The Devil
The decisive break with sin through faith	The world

In each case, Scripture assures us that the powers which are for us are far greater than those ranged against us. The victory is secure. But the height of the battle is joined when God summons us to put sin to death.

DEALING WITH SIN

Our forefathers used to speak of mortifying sin. That may conjure up ideas of men of reclusive instincts flaying their bodies in the hope of avoiding sin. We know better from Scripture—the body may be the instrument of sin, but it is not its source, and therefore to deal harshly with it is no solution to the problem. 'The flesh' is not merely 'flesh and blood'! But these mediaeval associations have tended to persuade Christians that the whole idea of putting sin to death is somehow or another related to legalism and the righteousness of the law.

We must affirm in this context that crucifying sin is a central practical issue in Christian experience. This neglected area of truth must be recovered, and in our present culture must be taught to younger and older Christians alike. Undoubtedly one of the reasons some younger Christians make shipwreck of their faith is because they have never learned how to deal with indwelling sin, or, what is worse, have been encouraged to see it as an irrelevance. It is one of the signs of our morally-confused church life today that there is so much hesitation here. We have lost confidence in the clear commands of Scripture.

The word 'mortify' appears relatively infrequently, even in the older Bible translations. But the idea of dealing radically with sin is liberally spread throughout the New Testament. Our Lord speaks of its necessity in the Sermon on the Mount:

> If your right eye causes you to sin, gouge it out and throw it away. It is better for you to lose one part of your body than for your whole body to be thrown into hell. And if your right hand causes you to sin, cut it off and throw it away. It is better for you to lose one part of your body than for your whole body to go into hell.
>
> Matthew 5:29–30

The same idea is present when he tells us that if we are to be his disciples, we must deny ourselves, take up the Cross and follow him. In the Gospels, as in the Letters, the Cross was the most vivid symbol-word for death. To follow Christ *means* to pronounce the death-sentence upon sin and to be in process of putting that sentence into effect by a daily crucifixion of all that sets itself against God's purposes in our lives. Inevitably, as Jesus himself seems to indicate by the conditional nature of his words in the Sermon (*If* your right eye causes you to sin . . .), the sources of our temptations differ according to our personalities, temperaments and circumstances. Each of us has to learn, often the hard way, where our own personal areas of weakness lie. But the necessity to mortify sin, however it makes its presence felt, is universal. *No man can be Christ's disciple without daily carrying the Cross.* Those who belong to Christ have crucified the flesh with its lusts (Gal. 5:24).

In fact in the New Testament this very practical question of *how* to put sin to death was being discussed, and long before the later eras of church history false teaching was already being propounded. The letter to the Colossians in particular is to be read against this background. Some false teachers were enforcing special regulations in the church. Certain things were not to be eaten, other items were taboo—'this is the way to deal with sin and go on to a life of holiness and "perfection" ' was the assurance which was being canvassed. But Paul cuts through this humbug in his devastating fashion:

> Such regulations indeed have an appearance of wisdom, with their self-imposed worship, their false humility and their harsh treatment of the body, *but they lack any value in restraining sensual indulgence.*
> Colossians 2:23

Clearly Paul is attempting to do two things for the Colossians in this passage: *firstly*, to lay a proper foundation *in the grace of God* to help us to deal with sin, and *secondly*, to expound the practical implications of putting sin to death.

The Foundation

The Colossians were being urged to crucify sin on an entirely mistaken basis. Paul speaks of them being taken captive 'through hollow and deceptive philosophy, which depends on human tradition and the basic principles of this world *rather* than on Christ' (Col. 2:8). John Owen put his finger on the issue in the standard evangelical work on this theme (significantly, originally sermons to teen-age boys), when he wrote: 'Mortification from a self-strength, carried on by ways of self-invention unto the end of self-righteousness, is the soul and substance of all false religion in the world.' If we build it on man-made rules (don't do this, don't go to that, don't touch this, keep away from that) we live under the delusion that we are truly dealing with indwelling sin when in fact we are merely altering our outward habits. This is no lasting foundation, and when the crisis of the 'day of evil' comes (Eph. 6:13) we will find ourselves on sinking sand.

The true foundation for dealing with sin is union with Christ. Already we have seen the general nature of this union (in chapter 11), and one area in which it has practical repercussions (in chapter 13). Now Paul brings these two elements together, and shows how the extensive nature of our union with Christ—we have died with him (Col. 2:20; 3:3); we have been raised with him (3:1); we have our present lives hidden with him in his heavenly reign (3:3); and we will be inseparably united with him in his coming (3:4)—is in fact the basis for slaying sin. His argument is that 'Since . . .' these things are true, 'therefore' we are to mortify whatever belongs to our earthly nature (Col. 3:1 and 5).

But what is the inner logic of this argument? It is (as we saw in Chapter 13) that our union with Christ gives us a new identity in which our relationship to sin is radically altered, and we are raised to a new dignified status in Christ. Since we are thus united to him the foundation has been laid for an entirely different way of life and a new devotion of our affections. Our new identity is itself the new incentive we need to deal with sin. Just as a newly-married bride is given a new name and with it a completely new identity, that new identity is the only incentive she needs to live a life in which her affections are entirely set upon her husband. Beforehand she may have felt varying degrees of affection towards others. Now her husband must have a unique affection, and anything that would tend to mar, distort or destroy that affection must be rigorously and consistently refused. So with those who are married to Christ by grace and faith (cf. Rom. 7:4).

Put sin to death'

We must, however, be a little more explicit. Up until now we have used Paul's expression 'put to death' without defining it. But what exactly does it mean?

It is in some ways easier to say what it is not. It is not the eradication of sin. No Christian ever comes to the place in this life where he has so completely destroyed indwelling sin that it no longer exists (1 Jn. 1:8). For such a deliverance we must wait. Nor is putting sin to death the same thing as diverting it. Sometimes when men grow older the external circumstances and pattern of their lives may change to such an extent that the 'old' sins no longer trouble them. But to assume they are dead is to fall into the same fatal trap as the man who thinks himself free from his alcoholism when he has become so numbed by drink that all desires have gone except the desire for sleep. Nor does Paul mean by 'put to death' to be driven by fear of discovery to divert our sinful habits into another, more socially acceptable, less readily discoverable *form* of sin. Altering sin's *form* does not change its *nature*. This is not putting sin to death. Nor is it simply a quiet and peaceful temperament, nor being interested in 'intellectual' rather than 'physical' matters. It is clear in the New Testament that most of the 'sins of the flesh' are mental rather than physical.

What then is this killing of sin? It is the constant battle against sin which we fight daily—the refusal to allow the eye to wander, the mind to contemplate, the affections to run after anything which will draw us from Christ. It is the deliberate rejection of any sinful thought, suggestion, desire, aspiration, deed, circumstance or provocation at the moment we become conscious of its existence. It is the consistent endeavour to do all in our powers to weaken the grip which sin in general, and its manifestations in our own lives in particular, has. It is not accomplished only by saying 'no' to what is wrong, but by a determined acceptance of all the good and spiritually-nourishing disciplines of the gospel. It is by resolutely weeding the garden of the heart, *and also* by planting, watering and nurturing Christian graces there, that putting sin to death will take place. Not only must we slay the noxious weeds of sin, but we must see that the flowers of grace are sucking up the nourishment of the Spirit's presence in our hearts. Only when those hearts are so full of grace will less room exist for sin to breathe and flourish.

Colossians 3:5-11 is particularly interesting here, because it gives us a helpfully concise summary of the areas of Christian experience in which we need to deal with sin. Between the lines we may read some of the ways in which that sin is to be mortified:

> Put to death, therefore, whatever belongs to your earthly nature: sexual immorality, impurity, lust, evil desires and greed which is idolatry. Because of these the wrath of God is coming. You used to walk in these ways, in the life you once lived. But now you must rid yourselves of all such things as these: anger, rage, malice, slander and filthy language from your lips. Do not lie to each other, since you have taken off your old self with its practices and have put on the new self, which is being renewed in knowledge in the image of its Creator. Here there is no Greek or Jew, circumcised or uncircumcised, barbarian, Scythian, slave or free, but Christ is all, and is in all.

WHERE?

Paul seems to indicate the importance of mortification in the three concentric circles of experience in which every Christian is at the centre.

(i) In our private lives

The list of what belongs to the earthly nature in v. 5 deals largely with inward motivation as well as external conduct. Our hearts are universes of their own, and out of them emerge all kinds of evil. Paul brings out into the open at this point sinful desires and acts of which we rarely speak. That is not a justification for sexual impurity and lust becoming a regular part of our conversation. Indeed, in his parallel letter to the Ephesians he regards such conversation as 'unwholesome' (Eph. 4:29). But he mentions these things here because this is the area in which many Christians face their severest tests. It is of no value to pretend that such painful temptations do not exist. The saintly Robert Murray M'Cheyne once wrote in his diary that he had discovered that the seed of every known sin was dwelling in his heart. Sometimes it is impossible for us really to make progress in holiness until we realise that—*and until we specify to ourselves and before God what our own sins are*. Ashamed as we are, if 'dirty-mindedness' (J. B. Phillips' translation) is a real problem for us, we must face up to it, and nail it to the Cross of Christ: lust and greed must be similarly treated.

(ii) In our everyday experiences

In v. 8, Paul goes on to list characteristics which tend to be revealed at home and work. Anger and rage! A spirit of malice—rejoicing in the mishaps of others of whom we are jealous, or whom we are just 'plain agin' (against, antagonistic to). Can Christians use filthy language? The possibility was not beyond Paul's imagination. 'But now you must rid yourselves of all such things as these' (v. 8). R. C. H. Lenski suggests in his *Commentary on Colossians* that we should translate 'rage' by 'exasperation'. How that hits home! Sometimes men have looked upon such impatience as being a Christian virtue. No, says Paul, kill it!

(iii) In the fellowship of the church

In the fellowship of the redeemed there must be a consistent refusal to yield to elements in our own hearts which will engender disruption and strife within the fellowship. 'Do not lie to each other' (v. 9). This is the negative expression of the parallel statement in Ephesians 4:15 where, literally, we are told to 'truth it to one another'. Not merely speak the truth, but live truthfully, openly and honestly with one another. 'Do not live a lie!' is what Paul is saying. Nor are we to make capital out of our background. In those days the church was composed of Jews and Gentiles, cultured and uncultured, slaves and free men. Today it is at least as diversified. But those differences are meant to serve the cause of unity, and the unity of such different people is meant to serve the cause of evangelism (Jn. 17:23). Therefore any assumption of superiority which is based on intelligence, 'old school tie' mentality, the area of town in which we live, the kind of clothes we wear, the tones of our accents, is anathema in the house of God. It must be dragged to the Cross and brutally slain for the sake of Christ who loved the church and gave himself for it. Rich though he was, he became poor for its sake, and being made poor, died as an outcast in society for the unity of the fellowship of God's people. Whether in the mind only, in the impressions we give, or in actual deed and word, these crimes against the seamless robe of Christ must be met with the nails of crucifixion!

How?

As we read between the lines and catch the spirit of Paul's teaching in Colossians 3 we see that Paul also indicates some practical steps we can take in order to put sin to death. From what he says there are five 'principles' which we might draw up:

(i) Recognise sin for what it is (Col. 3:5, 8, 11)

Psychiatrists sometimes distinguish between what they call *suppression* and *repression*. Suppression involves rejecting the opportunity to do something and repression means denying that we want to do it. The first of these, we are assured, is a normal, healthy activity (indeed, certainly for the Christian, it is a necessary activity). But the second leads to all manner of psychological disorder. In the life of the Christian that disorder will penetrate from his psychological to his spiritual condition, with disastrous consequences. No doubt there are subtle pressures upon us to appear to be better than we are, but to give way to them by repression is fatal. No doubt too, Satan will want to make as much capital out of our indwelling sin as he can—who has not encountered his accusation, 'how can you be a Christian with such thoughts as these passing through your mind?' How easily, just then, we lose our grasp of the fact that salvation is *by grace* not by works, and justification is *by faith* and not by personal righteousness, and that it is *Christ*, not ourselves, who saves us. However daring it sounds under other circumstances, under these circumstances we must even dare to say: 'But I can never be more justified than I am at this very moment—even with these thoughts and desires – for I am still trusting in Christ, and by his grace these sins will be put to death.' But only as we face up to them and see them in their full ugliness will we recognise that crucifixion must be their fate.

(ii) Bring your sin into the light of God's presence

The last thing we naturally do must be the first thing we spiritually do. 'Because of these the wrath of God is coming' is Paul's word about our sins (Col. 3:6). To see my sin clearly, to motivate my heart to be quit with it, I must take it to where I see it in the light of God's wrath against all ungodliness and unrighteousness (Rom. 1:18). That place is the Cross. In my mind's eye let me take my sin there, and in the darkness of that afternoon outside the gate of the city of Jerusalem, let me witness the reproach of Christ. Let me see the Sun darken for shame, the onlookers leave wailing and beating their breasts (Lk. 23:48), and let me hear the cry of the Wrath-Bearer: 'My God, my God, why have you forsaken me?' Let me look at my sin, and penitently say, 'Lord Jesus, the answer lies *here*, in this sin that caused you such pain.' We cannot go that far and *not* want to put sin to death.

(iii) Recall the shame of past sin
'You used to walk in these ways, in the life you once lived' (Col. 3:7). That is what we might call 'the comparative principle' in Christian living. On some occasions it is an unhealthy thing to be looking back and taking our spiritual temperature. But in these circumstances this may prove to be a means of grace. 'What benefit did you reap at that time from the things you are now ashamed of?' asks Paul (Rom. 6:21). It is the same principle here. Why return to the old manner of life, when you have entered into the joys of eternal life? Why live as the 'old man', when in Christ the old has passed away?

(iv) Remember you are united to Christ
Paul had already expounded this in vv. 1–4. It is hinted at again in vv. 9–10. The 'old self' and 'new self' (literally old and new 'man') are almost technical expressions in the New Testament. The 'old man' is what we were by nature in union with Adam. The 'new man' is what we have become in Christ by virtue of our union with him. 'Remember who you are in Christ,' is what Paul is saying, 'and let that knowledge do its powerful work throughout your lives. Remember that you are indissolubly united to Christ.' This is the motivation he uses elsewhere, in 1 Corinthians 6:17, where he says, in effect, that even when we sin we do not separate ourselves from Christ. We may distance ourselves from a sense of his presence, but we

remain one with him—so that in fact, when we sin, *we drag Christ into our sin.* 'Do you not know that your bodies are members of Christ himself?' (1 Cor. 6:15).

(v) Prayerfully seek the fruit of the Spirit

This is the point of the many positive exhortations which follow (see Col. 3:12-17). 'Grace is to corruption as water is to fire,' wrote John Flavel. If we sow to the Spirit, we will reap from the Spirit. If, through the Spirit we put to death the deeds of the sinful flesh, there is a promise given that we shall live (Rom. 8:13). Our great need therefore is for *perseverance.*

16
Perseverance

Christians of all theological persuasions and of none have cheerfully sung with the converted slave-trader John Newton:

> *Amazing grace! how sweet the sound*
> *That saved a wretch like me!*
> *I once was lost, but now am found:*
> *Was blind, but now I see.*

Our studies thus far have tried to catch Newton's theme as it is expressed in biblical teaching. The amazing thing about grace is that it has saved me; the thing which keeps me amazed by grace is the contrast between what I was (lost, blind) and what I have become in Christ (found, sighted). In a variety of ways we have noticed that this is a recurring theme in the New Testament. But this spirit of amazement takes hold only of these who have gained some appreciation of what God has done in bringing them into his kingdom.

Another verse in Newton's famous hymn reminds us that the work which God has begun in our lives is one which he means to complete:

> *Through many dangers, toils and snares*
> *I have already come:*
> *'Tis grace that brought me safe thus far,*
> *And grace will lead me home.*

There are, however, many reasons for asking whether Newton had got things right or not. After all, we have just been examining the conflicts in which every Christian eventually finds himself engaged, with the world, the flesh and the devil. It seems— at least from that perspective—a little premature to sing with Newton that 'grace will lead me home'. Certainly singing that with the cheerfulness and hearty voice we associate with these lines hardly seems at first glance to be in keeping with the battles we have to fight in the Christian life. Had Newton taken the 'many dangers, toils and snares' of the Christian's experience a little more seriously, would he have written quite so confidently?

The question this raises for us is, of course, that of perseverance. How can I be sure that, having started on the Christian way, I am going to arrive at the goal? If as John Bunyan suggests in the *Pilgrim's Progress*, there is a road leading to condemnation even from the very gates of the celestial city, where am I likely to find the confidence that I will persevere to the end? Not only so, but when we turn from the pastoral drama of *Pilgrim's Progress* to the pastoral realities of the past and present life of the church we do not need to look far for illustrations of failure to persevere. In the sixteenth century, when the Reformation was progressing in Italy, a lawyer from the town of Cittadella in the state of Venice, who had embraced the faith of the Reformation, appeared before the Inquisition, denied the faith he had confessed, made a public recantation, and died later in the same year, 1548, in a state of deep melancholy in the conviction that he had committed the unpardonable sin. His life would have no importance at all were it not for the fact that, through his biographers' accounts of those dark days, many evangelical preachers in the following century in England made frequent reference to the awesome possibility of failing to persevere, and illustrated it from the life of this man, *Francis Spira*. John Bunyan, describing his own spiritual progress in his autobiographical *Grace Abounding to the Chief of Sinners*, tells of the consequences in his own life of reading about Spira:

> darkness and despair were swallowing me up ... God has let me fall, my sin is unpardonable ... About this time I did light on that dreadful story of that miserable mortal Francis Spira, a book that was to my troubled spirit as salt when rubbed in a fresh wound—every sentence in that book, every groan of that man ... Especially that sentence of his was frightful to me: 'Man knows the beginning of sin, but who bounds the issues thereof?' Sometimes I could, for whole days together, feel my very body, as well as my mind, to shake and totter under the sense of this dreadful judgment of God that should fall on those that have sinned ...
> *Grace Abounding* section 163

We must therefore face the question which presses in on us

also from the unhappy ending which some of our own contemporaries may have made to their spiritual pilgrimage: *if this can happen, how do I know it will not happen to me?* This is the problem of *perseverance*.

The New Testament warns us by precept and example that some professing Christians may not persevere in their profession of Christ to the end of their lives. It was possible for a member of the band of disciples who accompanied Jesus to fail precisely here, with the most terrible consequences. It seems also that more than one of Paul's companions not only deserted him, but deserted Christ as well. We cannot therefore assume that the antidote to such tendencies will be easily found. Jesus seems to indicate the reverse in his parable of the Sower and the soils, in which only one of the categories of hearers bears fruit and perseveres. All the others are eventually swallowed up and destroyed by the malignant influences which militate against Christian perseverance. It is this general background that gives point to the example Paul set his fellow-Christians in Corinth:

> I do not run like a man running aimlessly; I do not fight like a man beating the air. No, I beat my body and make it my slave so that after I have preached to others, I myself will not be disqualified for the prize.
> 1 Corinthians 6:26–7

Similarly, when we read through the Letter to the Hebrews, we cannot but be struck, even astonished, by the way it is so regularly punctuated by words of warning and exhortation to persevere. This was clearly a matter of unusual concern for the writers of the New Testament.

Yet, on the other hand, there are strong, almost extreme assurances given to believers in the same New Testament, which appear to stress the absolute certainty of Christian perseverance and lend weight to Newton's confidence that no amount of future danger will prevent the Christian from running the race to the very end. Did not the apostle Paul who kept his body in subjection lest he be disqualified, also express unbounded confidence that at the end of the day he would receive the crown of life (2 Tim. 4:6–8)?

Assurances of Perseverance

It would be a mistake to think that the arguments which demonstrate the doctrine of the saints' perseverance are largely *logical* rather than *biblical*. We need look no further than the words of Jesus:

> My sheep listen to my voice; I know them, and they follow me. I give them eternal life, and they shall never perish; no-one can snatch them out of my hand. My Father, who has given them to me, is greater than all; no-one can snatch them out of my Father's hand. I and the Father are one.
>
> John 10:27-30

It is not easy to see how these words can be turned on their heads to suggest that the Bible gives us no assurance we will persevere. Nor is it good enough, in the face of such plain speaking by our Lord, to suggest that the doctrine of perseverance is not explicitly taught in Scripture, but is a deduction from it. Nothing could be plainer than the language which Jesus used in John 10.

Similar affirmations occur in Paul's letters. To the Philippians he writes that he is 'confident of this, that he who began a good work in you will carry it on to completion until the day of Christ Jesus' (Phil. 1:6). Admittedly he is speaking there in a corporate, not an individual context—but that context must of necessity include the experience of individuals. Certainly it is of individuals he speaks in his climactic words at the end of Romans 8, where, challenging all the powers on earth, in heaven, and under the earth, he speaks of the certainty he has that nothing can separate God's children from Christ's love. The basis of that certainty he had earlier expounded in the chain of saving acts which bring all the called through justification to glorification. There is no hint here that God's purposes may be foiled or that anything can ever break 'the sacred chain that binds the earth to heaven above'. God did not spare his own Son but gave him up to the death of the Cross. It is unthinkable that he would withhold from us the grace we need to persevere. Christ's death, properly understood, guarantees perseverance. So runs Paul's argument in Romans 8:32.

The New Testament further focuses attention on a number of

important doctrinal considerations which persuade us that God enables his children to persevere, despite all opposition.

God has chosen us in Christ. All the blessings of the gospel flow from this fountain, and assume the necessity of perseverance. When God's choice is described as *predestination* the issue really seems to be beyond doubt unless the purpose of God is to fail. He has not only set his love on us but determined our eternal destiny as his people—a destiny, as Paul notes in the same paragraph, of glorification and therefore of perseverance. If this is true the child of God will certainly persevere, since God is persevering with him. He will be able to sing:

> *Faith hath an overcoming power,*
> *It triumphs in the dying hour:*
> *Christ is our life, our hope, our joy,*
> *Nor can our foes that hope destroy.*
>
> *Not all that men on earth can do,*
> *Nor powers on high, nor powers below,*
> *Shall cause his mercy to remove,*
> *Or wean our hearts from Christ our love.*
>
> Isaac Watts

Thus, according to Peter, through faith we are shielded by God's power for the inheritance which is reserved in heaven for us (1 Pet. 1:4–5). It may be objected that Peter emphasises the instrumentality of *faith* in perseverance. *There is no such thing in Scripture as perseverance without faith.* But Peter also says that those who have faith will persevere!

God indwells his people by the Spirit. Jesus promised that his Spirit, the Counsellor, is given 'to be with you for ever' (Jn. 14:16). Since he dwells in us, we may apply the confident tones of John's words to ourselves, that he who is in us is greater than he who is in the world. So Thomas Watson, working out the biblical affirmation that the Holy Spirit indwells believers, expresses it like this:

> He who dwells in a house, keeps the house in repair; so the Spirit dwelling in a believer, keeps grace in repair. Grace is compared to a river of the water of life, Jn. 7:38. This river can never be dried up, because God's Spirit is the spring that continually feeds it.
> *A Body of Divinity* (1890) p. 195

Christ intercedes for the Christian. This truth, much neglected in the church, is one which lies at the heart of the biblical doctrine of perseverance. Several times in Scripture the power of Christ's death is closely related to his continuing ministry as the High Priest of his people in prayer. Christ not only died, writes Paul, he was raised from the dead and is at God's right hand making intercession (Rom. 8:34). Indeed, writes the author of Hebrews, he lives for ever to intercede for us (Heb. 7:25; cf. 6:20). He is our heavenly advocate, says John, and in the great prayer of John 17 we find a true reflection of that intercessory ministry of our King and Lord. There our Lord's burden is, at least in part, for the preservation of his disciples so that they may persevere to the end and their witness may be preserved (Jn. 17:11, 15). It is this spirit which Charles Wesley (whose best theology appears in his hymns) caught in his fine hymn 'Wherewith, O God, shall I draw near?':

> *See where before the throne He stands,*
> *And pours the all-prevailing prayer,*
> *Points to His side, and lifts His hands,*
> *And shows that I am graven there.*
>
> *He ever lives for me to pray:*
> *He prays that I with Him may reign:*
> *Amen to what my Lord doth say!*
> *Jesus, Thou canst not pray in vain.*

Simon Peter's experience sets before us the practical pattern of such intercession. He denied Christ, and yet persevered despite such abysmal failure, precisely because his life was upheld by the intercessions of his Saviour before the throne of God. Jesus explains what the focus of his own praying is: 'Simon, Simon, Satan has asked to sift you as wheat. But I have prayed for you, Simon, that your faith may not fail' (Lk. 22:31-2). There is no separation even here of perseverance from faith. But Christ's petitions call down such aid to faith that it stands even in its darkest hour. Whenever we find our lives drawn into the snares of the devil as Peter did, we cannot rely on our own strength, nor even on our own faith, but only upon Christ's faithfulness in prayer for his weak brethren. That knowledge brings consolation. It also brings assurance that nothing will ever separate us from God's love in Christ.

Perseverance and faith, therefore, or perseverance and the Christian's duty to battle on in the fight of faith, are never separated and polarised in the Bible. It is never a case of 'either/or', always one of 'both/and'. In fact we persevere through faith and never apart from it. The picture is one of a dynamic, living trust in a God who actively holds on to us so that we may persevere. There is no blanket guarantee of perseverance. There is no mere doctrine of 'the security' of the believer, as though God's keeping of us took place irrespective of the lives we live. Indeed there is no such thing in the New Testament as a believer whose perseverance is so guaranteed that he can afford to ignore the warning notes which are sounded so frequently. No early Christian was more concerned lest he become a spiritual castaway than the man who had proved the perseverance of his own faith when he had been a literal castaway and discovered that not even nakedness, peril or sword could destroy the love of Christ for him.

But it is never enough to fix our gaze only on the assurance which we find in Scripture. We must give our attention to two other matters: the *hindrances* which persevering Christians must face, and the *means* which God has ordained for our continuing in the faith.

Hindrances to Perseverance

Jesus addressed himself to this issue in the parable of the Sower and the soils, when he uncovered the various heart-responses we can make to his word. We can either stifle its influences (so that even if we appear to have begun as Christians, we do not continue), or let it work fruitfully in our hearts.

There is the hindrance of a heart which does not allow the word of God to penetrate, and is therefore easy prey for Satan. Some people never really persevere because they have never even begun to allow divine truth to break up the hardened soil of their lives. Jesus spoke of this under the figure of the pathway. It is a strange thought that in the parable, the pathway was probably the area on which the sower himself would have walked seed-time after seed-time. The spiritual parallel is no less enigmatic: many people are hardened in their hearts by the very activity of listening to the word of God but not hearing it *with faith* (cf. Heb. 4:2). In the lives of such it has no opportunity to 'bear fruit and prevail'.

The second possibility is 'rocky soil'. Such hear the word of life, receiving it 'with joy', and at once spring up. But Jesus significantly adds that when troubles and difficulties appear on the horizon they wither and die, *since they have no root*. To receive the word of God *only with joy* is a common sign of someone who may well never really persevere. In pastoral situations it is invariably a warning sign and a cause of some anxiety to those who have a care for us. For biblical teaching suggests that we truly respond to the message of the gospel only when our hearts experience *both joy and sorrow*. Even from a psychological point of view it is not possible for sinful men and women to rejoice in the forgiveness of sins and life everlasting without knowing some kind of sorrow for what they are and have been. Similarly in developing Christian experience we cannot separate the rhythm of sorrow and joy which is so often stressed in the New Testament. Christians in this world are 'sorrowful, yet always rejoicing' (2 Cor. 6:10); but never one without the other—at least in this world.

The trouble with this kind of person, Jesus seems to be saying, is that they have grasped only half a gospel, and half a foundation is no security to us when the winds begin to howl, and the storm of persecution breaks over our heads. If we think that Christian living is all joy and happiness, we are heading for a rude awakening.

The third cause of failure to persevere is located in what our Lord calls the thorny soil. What are the thorns? They are 'the worries of this life, the deceitfulness of wealth and the desires for other things' (Mk. 4:19). These 'choke the word, making it unfruitful'. It is important to notice how this application of Jesus' teaching applies to all strata of society. It is by no means confined to the rich, or to the poor, to the intelligent or to those of little understanding. All of us, whatever our abilities and place in society, may know the worries of this life, the feeling that 'the grass is greener on the other side' (even millionaires know that experience!). But these influences are fatal to the influence of God's word on the human heart, and will choke it.

Undoubtedly we ought to apply these principles all of the

time to the whole of our lives. These are hindrances to perseverance. But Jesus is emphasising that these are features of our hearts which we have failed to deal with *from the beginnings of our reception of God's word.* Their *effects* may appear later on, but the reason they ruin any likelihood of our perseverance is that they were not rooted out from the start. It has always been true in the Christian life that a great deal of difficulty stems from a bad beginning. Often the only solution is to go back to the roots, to make sure they are clean, to use our spiritual weed-killer on what we have allowed into our hearts from early on in Christian experience. Otherwise we may discover, as the parable suggests, that we have allowed into our hearts so much that is inimical to God's purpose that there has really been no real room for God himself. There is only one sure guarantee of perseverance:

> But the seed on good soil stands for those with a noble and good heart, who hear the word, retain it, and by persevering produce a crop.
>
> Luke 8:15

The question then is: How do we get such hearts which retain the word, and *by persevering* produce a crop?

The Means of Perseverance

There is probably no stronger encouragement to us to persevere than the knowledge that God is persevering with us. We are often tempted to turn in upon ourselves. Then we need to turn out towards God and the many assurances we find in his word that he will never leave us and never forsake us; that we are in the hands of Christ and his Father's hands give us double protection and hold us up:

> *'Twixt gleams of joy and clouds of doubt*
> *Our feelings come and go;*
> *Our best estate is tossed about*
> *In ceaseless ebb and flow.*
> *No mood of feeling, form of thought,*
> *Is constant for a day;*
> *But thou, O Lord, thou changest not:*
> *The same thou art alway.*

> *I grasp thy strength, make it mine own,*
> *My heart with peace is blest;*
> *I lose my hold, and then comes down*
> *Darkness, and cold unrest.*
> *Let me no more my comfort draw*
> *From my frail hold of thee,*
> *In this alone rejoice with awe—*
> *Thy mighty grasp of me.*
>
> *Out of that weak, unquiet drift*
> *That comes but to depart,*
> *To that pure heaven my spirit lift*
> *Where thou unchanging art.*
> *Lay hold of me with thy strong grasp,*
> *Let thy almighty arm*
> *In its embrace my weakness clasp,*
> *And I shall fear no harm.*
>
> *Thy purpose of eternal good*
> *Let me but surely know;*
> *On this I'll lean—let changing mood*
> *And feeling come or go—*
> *Glad when thy sunshine fills my soul,*
> *Not lorn when clouds o'ercast,*
> *Since thou within thy sure control*
> *Of love dost hold me fast.*
>
> John Campbell Shairp

But this is not the whole of the New Testament's teaching. For God not only works sovereignly in our lives, he also works through means. His perseverance *produces* our perseverance. He makes *provision* for us to persevere.

What then are these *means* provided by God to be employed by ourselves, which lead to Christian perseverance?

The first is obviously *the word of God*. We hide it in our hearts to prevent us from sinning (Ps. 119:11). It contains many notes of warning, and these stir us to press on in faith. It explains to us the pattern of God's purposes, and this gives us heart when we go through periods of trial or days of spiritual dryness. It provides us with 'great and precious promises' from God (2 Pet. 1:4) to encourage and assure us as we battle on for Christ. It was something of this which was part of Peter's nightmare experience during the hours of Christ's passion. He had denied his Lord; he seemed to be on the verge of committing apostasy; he was under strong satanic attack. But he 'remembered the word the Lord had spoken' (Lk. 22:61) which not only smote his conscience and awakened it from slumber, causing him to weep penitential tears, but must also have brought to mind that other word of promise, 'I have prayed for you, Simon, that your faith may not fail' (Lk. 22:32). Here was the word of Christ performing its twofold function in tilling the soil of Peter's heart, weeding out the thorns, *and* establishing him for the future. Before with joy alone he responded to Christ. Was there a laugh in his voice when he declared: 'These others may fall away, but not I'? Now there was sorrow, as Christ's word tore out the thorns of pride and self-sufficiency. Now there was true joy, born out of the tears of repentance. In this way God's word is the great means of preservation and perseverance, and as the Spirit of God, the Strengthener, continues to employ it, so we press on against any odds in the service of Christ.

The second means by which we persevere is that of *obedience to duties*. The very idea of 'duty' in the Christian life has gone into abeyance in recent decades. But it is much in need of reviving. More failure in Christian living can be traced to this than almost anything else. When we go 'off the rails' spiritually, the rails we leave are those of our duties. From the first sin of Genesis 3 in which Adam and Eve failed in their duties to God and to one another, through the gross sin of David in 2 Samuel 11–12, when David left his kingly duties (it was 'the time when kings go off to war' 2 Sam. 11:1) and took instead to a life of ease, until the present day, perhaps more spiritual disaster is caused by failure here than in any other area. Of course nothing is more tempting when we go through 'the blues' than to neglect prayer and God's word, witnessing and worship. But nothing is so rapidly calculated to lead to increasing lethargy. It is incumbent upon us therefore, in season and out of season, to bind to our consciences the duties of our individual Christian life.

The third means is that of *Christian fellowship*. Preachers of previous generations liked to use the illustration of a live coal separated from the others in a fire—gradually losing its heat and becoming dead. Even for centrally-heated Christians the picture still conveys a good deal! God has so constituted us as Christians that to be what God intends we *need* fellowship. Worshipping, praying, witnessing with others, having social interaction on mental and spiritual levels and even in the general gifts of God's grace, are some of the means God has promised to employ to keep us 'marching to Zion'. Such passages as Romans 12, Ephesians 4, 1 Corinthians 12–14 show us that our spiritual progress depends in measure on our being able to minister *to* others, and our receiving ministry *from* others. We are members of a body, says Paul—and the body moves, lives and grows *together*. That is why the normal pattern for our lives is that we belong to a living, praying, worshipping company of God's people.

God has provided these blessings for our perseverance in the faith. When they are providentially removed from us for a season we become only too aware of the vital role they play in our Christian lives. Let us not, therefore, despise these means of grace. They enable us to persevere to the end.

17
Asleep in Christ

Death! We do not normally regard dying as an aspect of Christian living. Death, after all, *overtakes* us, and we do not think of it as something we are to accomplish by the grace of God. Nor do we normally think of death as a biblical doctrine which carries practical repercussions for the Christian. To be frank, it is not a subject to which contemporary Christians give much sympathetic thought. It runs too obviously counter to the spirit of our times, and to think about it at all is to be accused (or even to accuse oneself!) of 'morbidity'.

Nevertheless, a moment's reflection teaches us that 'death' does have a place in the Christian life, and in fact marks one of the great crisis and transition points in its development.

We have already seen that God's work in our lives is, generally speaking, long-term and progressive, rather than sudden and critical. But we have noticed also that the Christian life is punctuated by crises. It begins with the great crisis of regeneration with its inherent sanctifying power in which we are set free once-for-all from the reign of sin. The ensuing struggle which we experience is a long-drawn-out process of warfare against the world, the flesh and the devil. But that struggle has an end. It does not continue for the Christian beyond the grave. The last crisis of death brings us into a new dimension altogether. We will see in the final chapter that in terms of the restoration of the image of God, death is not quite the end. There is more yet to come. That is why the primary hope of the Christian is not for death but for the return of the Lord Jesus Christ in majesty and glory. *Then* comes the end! But if Christ does not return during our lives, death will make for us the last staging-point before the grand finale of salvation. It is important then that we should think about it, that we should have some understanding of the biblical teaching on it, and that we should be equipped to die in Christ and for his glory.

The Nature of Death

The amazing advances of medical science and technology during the last decades have raised difficult practical and ethical issues for the medical profession in their understanding of 'the point of death'. Nor have these advances begun to take the mystery out of death itself. In some ways they have magnified the mystery all the more. Any reader who has been bereaved will not have forgotten the unique mystery about the sight of a body of someone known and loved. The difference between a dying man (even one who is weakness itself) and a dead man is infinite. The awesome sense that the 'person' is no longer there and has 'gone' is beyond description. Since we know one another only through the physical body in which we express our personality, it is not surprising that we should be stunned by the difference. For some of us it is really only at such times that we truly begin to learn that people are more than bodies. There is something about us that transcends the merely physical.

But all this is characteristic of our shared human experiences. What does Scripture have to teach us about death? What does death mean for the Christian?

The Bible teaches us that death is the consequence of sin. In the central passage in the Letter to the Romans, Paul explains man's condition on a cosmic scale by pointing to the sin of the first man. Through his sin death entered the world, and spread to all men—because all men had a share in his sin and were represented by him as their head in his act of rebellion against God (Rom. 5:12-21). That is why Paul says that death reigned even over those whose sin was not like that of Adam. Is that the Bible's explanation for the death of even infants who have never voluntarily and intelligently sinned? Certainly our forefathers thought so. Sin's wages are death, and are meted out equally to all, without discrimination.

Moreover in Scripture, death is regarded as part of the curse of sin. Death is not what we sometimes mistakenly suggest it is—a blessing, a release, a peaceful end. All of these may be found by the Christian in and through death, but they are in fact contrary to the true nature of death. For death is disintegration. It is the breaking of a union which God created. In and of itself it is an ugly, destructive thing—it is 'the last *enemy*'.

How is this so? Because death severs us from those we love. It breaks the cords that have joined us physically, mentally, spiritually to others. It deprives us of the most precious possessions we have on earth. The death of others separates us from them and places them in realms with which we are unable to communicate. My death means that I leave behind those to whom I have committed the whole of my life in love and devotion. In a sense I am being torn from part of myself in being taken from husband or wife, son or daughter, parent or brother.

There is yet another sundering in death. Not only am I to be separated from part of myself 'in a sense' by departing from my loved ones. I am myself to be broken—body from soul. This tent in which I have sojourned must be left behind (2 Cor. 5:1). The only instrument I have ever had by which to know myself and communicate with others will be separated from my eternal spirit—contrary to nature. That is a divorce of a magnitude beyond my frail understanding. Simply as a prospect it is a terrifying one. It is a curse! That is why, when our Lord contemplated death as it is in itself we read that his heart was filled with sorrow. The expressions which describe his psychological condition suggest that his whole being shuddered at the prospect of what was to take place in his own experience. The language used to describe his Gethsemane experience is of a 'confused, restless, half-distracted state, which is produced by physical derangement, or by mental distress, as grief, shame, disappointment' (J. B. Lightfoot, *Philippians*, p. 123). No wonder Luther commented, 'No man ever feared death like this man.'

So we discover the real nature of death only when we look at Christ. In other men we see varying responses, from fear to carelessness, sorrow to glad anticipation, and these responses are largely determined by the prospect men have *beyond* death. But when oour Lord contemplates death itself, he recoils at the sight. When he sees what it is that he is to carry on his own shoulders by dying, he asks God that such a cup might pass from him. We should not therefore lose sight of what death itself is. It is the destroyer of the life which God gave to man in his infinite love for him. It is therefore not only our last enemy, but God's enemy also.

The Death of Death

While all that we have said is true and biblical, it is not, at least for the Christian, the whole truth. For the Christian does not contemplate death in itself. He now sees it, as he sees all things, 'in Christ'. In itself it is an experience from which to turn completely. But in Christ the necessity of death takes on a new perspective. *That is why in the New Testament when we read of death it is usually of its defeat.* It is this which explains the triumph of the martyrs in the face of death, and the equanimity with which Christians great and small have faced it. In the face of a *defeated* foe we find, for example, that the early Methodists could take courage that their 'people died well'. If we would share that experience it is imperative that we know how and why death is for the Christian a defeated foe.

> *O Death, we defy thee!*
> *A stronger than thou*
> *Hath entered thy palace;*
> *We fear thee not now!*

In what way has Christ entered the palace of death and robbed it of its power? Scripture provides us with several answers.

(1) Christ came in our flesh in order to taste and share our death. The emphasis of the Letter to the Hebrews is that Christ became like us, in weakness, temptation and suffering in order to die. In doing so he became the 'pioneer' of our salvation (Heb. 2:10). He was raised from the dead by his Father in order to be a living Saviour and friend to his people, and as such has promised never to leave me and never to forsake me (Heb. 13:5). Had he done nothing else that would still make death a defeated enemy for me, because I know that when I walk through the valley of deep darkness or death, *he will be with me.* I will not be alone. In fact I will be accompanied by One who is the Resurrection and the Life. *We could call this our victory over the terrors of death.*

(ii) Christ has conquered 'him who holds the power of death' (Heb. 2:14). The word Hebrews uses is often translated 'destroy', and basically conveys the idea of rendering something inoperative, '*hors de combat*' as it were. The word *katargeō* is used in the parable of the unfruitful fig tree which 'cumbers' the ground (Lk. 13:7) in the sense of making the soil it is using quite unproductive. That is what Christ's death does to the powers of darkness (cf. 1 Cor. 2:6; 15:24). They are still in existence, but have been deprived of all authority. When (as they constantly seek to do) the powers of evil seek to invade the life of the believer *they have no authority to do so*, and therefore have to deceive the Christian into believing he is still under their dominion.

But how did Christ conquer Satan specifically as the one who 'holds the power of death'? What are the consequences of his victory? He did so by dealing with the basis for Satan's grip on our lives, namely sin. Paul tells us that by bearing our guilt and punishment on the cross, Christ was able to disarm the principalities and powers, to make a public example of them by triumphing over them in the Cross (Col. 2:15). The grip which the devil has on a Christian is weakened and broken as a consequence—we need not be under his thraldom. The primary consequence of this is that we may now be set free from our bondage to the fear of death! Since our guilt has been taken from us, and we are no longer children of wrath or servants of the ruler of this world (Eph. 2:1–4), the sting of death has been drawn for us by Christ (1 Cor. 15:55–7). *So long as we fix our gaze on the victory of Christ, we have nothing to fear.*

This, apparently, is why the New Testament thinks of death as sleep. (Not, as some Christians have occasionally thought, because the souls of Christians sleep between their death and the end of the world.) Death, when its sting is drawn and its powerful fears are rendered harmless, is but the means of our awakening on the morning of a new day in the presence of God. Despite all its power to terrify and bring us into bondage, death for the Christian whose faith is firmly fixed on Christ is but a sleep. It is, says Paul, a matter of the ship releasing its moorings, 'departing' from where our souls have been anchored in this world (Phil. 1:23), entering into the endless sea of Christ's nearer presence and being 'with Christ'. Who can doubt that this is 'far better'?

None of this is to deny that the individual Christian's experience of dying may be as diverse and inexplicable as our individual experience of sleep. By virtue of our complex psychological constitution some of us fall asleep with ease, almost at will, while others find entrusting themselves to sleep is a nightly battle. So it may be with death. There is no stereotyped pattern set before us in Scripture, for the experience of dying is also part of the means by which God prepares us for his presence. We can only stumblingly guess why it is that some Christians who have throughout their lives enjoyed large measures of assurance find the last battle is the greatest and that at times the sun's rays seem very dim, while others, who have been men of little confidence are blessed with an unusual sweetness and composure in their last hours. God is not confused by his own plans, purposes and manner of working, and into his hands we may confidently commit our spirits.

Preparation for Death

How then does the Christian view death? He learns to see it in its proper perspective. He does not lightly and superficially dismiss it. Nor does he allow his life to be paralysed by the fear of it. He recognises that death is an enemy, but he rejoices in the assurance that not even death can separate him from the love of Christ (Rom. 8:38) because in Christ its sting has been drawn, and although it may touch him (and, unless his Lord returns, *will*) it cannot harm him.

But even while this is the case, we have already noted that there is something unnatural about death, and therefore a sense in which the biblically-instructed Christian does not find it an easy matter to reconcile himself to it. It will be the destruction temporarily of all that he holds dear in this life, and he cannot *simpliciter* greet it as a friend. He must therefore engage in such spiritual exercises and disciplines as will enable him to sustain his heart when death approaches. Three of these exercises may be mentioned.

(i) We must set our hearts on Christ and the glory of his presence
This is what Paul did. He saw that to be with Christ was 'better by far' (Phil. 1:23). For while living was Christ for him, dying was gain—the gain of a more intimate and fulfilled knowledge of his Lord. That is something which is possible only for those who love

Christ now. If we prize him above all other things, and seek his kingdom and righteousness before everything else, then the prospect of actually seeing him face to face is one which will more than compensate for all that we may leave behind. Precisely *how* it will compensate we may not be able to say: but of this we can be sure, that the presence of the Son of God will be no disappointment.

Christians too are easily tempted away from this. How subtle a snare it is, for example, to suppose that so long as we cultivate our Christian service now, there will be time enough to cultivate a love for Christ and fellowship with him in later life. The great issues of our relationship with Jesus cannot wait until the angel of death approaches. For men usually die as they have lived. What we need to understand is that the habit of living at a low level of devotion to our Lord *is* a habit. It is neither easily broken at will, nor can its effects be readily repaired. It is not impossible, but it is relatively unlikely that we will be better Christians *then* than we want to be *now*. Preparation for the last day of Christian experience really begins on its first day.

(ii) We must remember the many blessings of the world to come

Christ is there. There also we will meet all those who are united to Christ. Those we have known: friends, ministers, elders, fathers, mothers, brothers and sisters—great and small who have helped us on our way. What a glorious thing the church in heaven must be, and what a privilege to come to that assembly of saints (Heb. 12:23)!

Undoubtedly we are out of our depth when we begin to think about these future joys, and there are so many questions which we ask and can only faintly answer. What will our relationships be like? How will we live without the pleasures we have known on earth, or those old relationships which were forged in our lives by God himself? Will those who have gone before us in youth or even in childhood somehow be matured? Will our knowledge of God come all at once, or will there be an ever-increasing understanding of his being? Will we recognise one another? Only one answer is possible to all these quite legitimate questions: in glory there will be no more curse. All will be joy and satisfaction, because God's blessing will flow without interruption to his people. Every joy we have known on earth will be seen to be but the shell of a blessing yet more concentrated. Everything will be real and lasting! But only in the experience of it will our questions vanish, and our lips confess: 'Now I understand' (1 Cor. 13:12). If we fix our minds on this assurance we will view our passing from this world into that which is to come in a new light.

(iii) We must learn to live now in the knowledge that this world is temporal

In other words we must live each day in the light of that day when we will be separated from this world. This is Paul's plea to the Corinthians which we noticed earlier in another connection. 'This world in its present form is passing away,' he writes, therefore 'those who use the things of the world' should live 'as if not engrossed in them' (1 Cor. 7:31). If we release our tight grip on all these things by holding fast primarily to Christ, then we will be better fitted to leave them all at the end of our lives, whether that end be sooner or later. When we learn to hold the world with a loose grip we are learning to take hold of the world to come with a firm grip. In this sense, as C. H. Spurgeon once pointed out in a sermon on Paul's words, 'I die daily' (1 Cor. 15:31):

> No man would find it difficult to die who died every day. He would have practised it so often, that he would only have to die but once more; like the singer who has been through his rehearsals, and is perfect in his part, and has but to pour forth the notes once for all, and have done. Happy are they who every morning go down to Jordan's brink, and wade into the stream in fellowship with Christ, dying in the Lord's death, being crucified on his cross, and raised in his resurrection. They, when they shall climb their Pisgah, shall behold nothing but what has been long familiar to them, as they have studied the map of death. . . . God teach us this art, and he shall have the glory of it. Amen.
> *Metropolitan Tabernacle Pulpit*, XIV, 491–2

Those who learn this grace may also rejoice in the prospect of sharing the experience of Bunyan's Mr Honest:

> When the day that he was to be gone was come, he addressed himself to go over the River. Now the River at that

time over-flow'd the banks in some places; But Mr Honest in his life-time had spoken to one Good-Conscience to meet him there, the which he also did, and lent him his hand, and so helped him over. The last words of Mr Honest were, *Grace Reigns*; So he left the World.

John Bunyan, *The Pilgrim's Progress*, pt. 2

'Then we shall see face to face' (1 Cor. 13:12).

18
Glorification

'Death is not the end'. Christians comfort themselves and one another with these words. They are, of course, true. Indeed they are more profoundly true than many Christians may themselves imagine when they say them. For not only does the New Testament point us to the glorious hope of the gospel in the world to come but it indicates to us that even when we die we have not yet been caught up in the events which the Bible regularly refers to as 'the end' (cf. Matt. 10:22; 24:13, 14; 1 Cor. 15:24; 1 Pet. 4:7). The goal of the Christian's vision is not his own death, but stretches beyond that to the return of Christ and the consummation of his kingdom. There is one last critical event to take place. This event, described variously and vividly in the Scriptures, is the last 'salvation-event' which has a decisive and critical influence on the life of the child of God. It takes us to the outer limits of Christian knowledge, and leaves us like men standing on the shore watching a boat disappear over the horizon into an experience at which we can only begin to guess. This event is our *glorification*.

In chapter 11 when we considered some of the dimensions of the Christian's union with Christ we noticed how extensive it is. The focus of that present union, however, lies in what Christ has done in the past, and what he is now accomplishing *on the basis of what he has done*. But we saw that there is one event in Christ's work yet to take place. In it the closeness of his union with his children will be more evidently seen than ever before. Paul expresses it in these terms:

> When Christ, who is your life, appears, then you also will appear with him in glory.
>
> Colossians 3:4

There are several fascinating features of this biblical teaching. If we are to have a fully-orbed picture of what it means to be a Christian we cannot afford to ignore them.

The reference in these words in Colossians is to the final

return of Christ which will be marked by the resurrection of the dead and the consummation of all things. In the New Testament that is the event which is marked by his glory. If this is so, then several emphases must be recognised.

The first is that while death brings the Christian into the immediate presence of God (to depart is to be with Christ, says Paul; 'To-day,' says Jesus to the penitent thief, 'you will be with me in paradise') God still has work to do in order to give to us the 'full salvation' about which we sometimes sing. Not only is that salvation not experienced to the full here and now; there is a sense in which it is not experienced even when we die. Not that dying for the Christian is ever anything less than 'gain' (Phil. 1:21). But God's clearly revealed purpose is not the salvation of 'souls', disembodied spirits who have at last rid themselves of the shackles of a body. That would not be salvation in the biblical sense, but only escape. Rather, God's purpose is to save men and women—and men and women enjoy *bodily*, not merely *spiritual* existence. The work of applying the finished work of Christ is therefore not complete until that day when the resurrection of our bodies has been accomplished by God.

Inevitably we have to think of these two events—death and resurrection—as separated by time. We know that time is not, however, the measure of eternity. We know that to think in these terms is, somehow or another, to simplify eternal reality. But, none the less, the Bible itself invites us to think even of the world to come in these categories of 'now and then', 'before and after' and we must do so. Glorious though the immediate presence of God must be, there is something greater still in store for us!

The second thing we must note is that there is also a sense in which something greater lies in store for Christ. The conversion of one person produces joy in heaven, and, if possible, that joy increases as heaven witnesses the powerful effect of Christ's work over the centuries. But there is yet more for heaven to witness. For the day is coming when the angels will be eye-witnesses to the return of Jesus. He will come to be glorified in the very world in which he was humiliated. How, or when, we do not know. But *that* he will come is fixed by the decree of God. Then every knee will bow to him and willingly or unwillingly confess his Lordship. His glory will be seen, and he will be glorified. *At that very moment Christians will share in his glory*, since they cannot ever be separated from him.

How this will happen is the third thing to note. It will happen because when Christ appears, Christians will be made like him, but not in the sense of only then being purified. As Christ rose from the dead on the first Easter, his soul and body having been separated but a matter of hours, so it will be with the Christian, even though his body and soul should have been rent asunder by death for centuries. Of course this is mysterious; of course it is an article of faith; of course it defies the laws of nature. But that is precisely the point. It is what we would expect. For the laws of nature participate in the effects of sin, and we would anticipate that when salvation is effected by Christ on a universal scale, the laws of nature also will be changed! At the end of the day there is nothing more amazing about the resurrection of the dead—even after centuries—than there is about the prototype resurrection of our Lord himself. *Then*, therefore, at the end of time only, will we really understand the significance of Paul's words that where sin abounded, grace abounds all the more. Only then will we, in the totality of our humanity, be 'like Christ'.

The fourth thing for us to note is the emphasis of the New Testament that this will take place in the experience of the whole church *at the same time*. What a tremendously exciting prospect this is! Here we are, at such different stages of Christian experience: some who have been Christians for many years, others converted recently; some highly gifted, others weak in both grace and gifts. Moreover, how many thousands and millions of God's children have passed out of this world before us? But *on that day* we will all together share in the glorification of Jesus, and our glorification with him. It is as though God has said to himself: 'I have given my children so much as individuals and as little groups; but now, in this last decisive act, in the public proclamation and appearance of my Son—I will give all of them my final special blessing all at once!' (See Col. 3:4; 1 Thess. 4:16 ff; 1 Jn. 3:2 for hints of this.)

But, we may well find ourselves asking, 'What will take place in glorification?' Besides these general emphases we have listed, the New Testament places four clearly-defined events before us.

(i) The resurrection

We have seen why the resurrection is necessary—because man is material and not just spiritual, and because Christ has set out to redeem and restore what has been broken and lost in man's sin. Just as the last great work of the Spirit in the life of Christ was his resurrection (cf. Rom. 1:4), so, in the application of Christ's work to us, the last influence of the Spirit is to do in us what he did first in Christ. This is the invariable direction of his activity, and it does not change or end before the resurrection.

It is unfortunate if we allow our minds to concentrate on the mysterious details of such an event. The very fact that it is a supernatural and unique event at the end of history inevitably means that we do not have the categories by which we can understand the mysteries involved. The only category we have by which to interpret it is the resurrection of Christ. That is our great assurance. Because he lives in resurrection power, we shall live. Because Christ having died once will never die again; because he lives in the power of an indestructible life, and because we are united to him—the power which once raised him from the dead will flow from him to raise up our mortal bodies (see Rom. 6:8–10; Heb. 7:16; Rom. 8:11). Paul puts the matter graphically at a period of his life when death seemed to loom large on the horizon (cf. Phil. 1:20–26; 2:17):

> Our citizenship is in heaven. And we eagerly await a Saviour from there, the Lord Jesus Christ, who, by the power that enables him to bring everything under his control, will transform our lowly bodies so that they will be like his glorious body.
>
> Philippians 3:20–1

The emphasis (consistently displayed throughout the New Testament) is on continuity as well as transformation. But the greater emphasis is on the marvellous transformation into a body of glory like Christ's from a 'lowly body'.

It should not be forgotten that the apostle Paul knew a little himself about longing for a regenerated body which would be a suitable vehicle for a renewed spirit; nor that he knew what it was to be so hampered by his body, through frailty, sickness and death. He knew what it was to have a 'thorn in the flesh' from which this life offered no release (2 Cor. 12:7–9). When he wrote to the Galatians his poor eyesight could be seen by the large letters he wrote reminding them of the time he had preached while suffering. They had taken him to their hearts in such a way that they would have gladly transplanted their eyes to him, were it then possible, to express their loving appreciation (Gal. 4:12-16). In other words he knew the kind of physical suffering which makes the Christian long that God would give him another body in which to live for his glory and honour. The good news of the gospel in this context is that the salvation it brings is physical as well as spiritual.

The day will come when the lame shall walk, the blind see, the deaf hear and the dead will rise. The body of lowliness in which we have lived and perhaps suffered will be changed into the likeness of Christ's.

(ii) The transformation

The change which will accompany the actual resurrection is also given prominent place in the teaching of the apostles. We will not merely be 're-embodied' as it were, but transformed in order to be like Christ. Involved in this final change will be the blossoming of the purpose God has had for us from the beginning. He predestined us, Paul says, to be conformed to the image of his Son (Rom. 8:29).

In the exposition of the resurrection in 1 Corinthians 15 Paul employs three analogies by which this transformation may be illuminated and measured.

(a) Like a seed planted in the ground and dying in order to produce the precious crop or flower, so our mortal bodies are planted in the earth in the sure and certain hope that they will be raised to a new form of life altogether. There is continuity, but there is also change; indeed such dramatic change that we can only wonder that the seed and the flower are related to one another. So it is with the resurrection body. It is transformed from the body of our death, although apparently (if Jesus' resurrection is to be the prototype) it remains recognisable (1 Cor. 15:25-39).

(b) Just as the bodies of created beings and objects differ, so the body of the resurrection will be different from the body of death. Take the planets, suggests the apostle; they have a different glory from the terrestrial bodies of animals, birds or fish. Again, the sun's body is different from that of the moon or stars in splendour. So there will be a dramatic change in the body of resurrection:

> The body that is sown is perishable, it is raised imperishable; it is sown in dishonour, it is raised in glory; it is sown in weakness, it is raised in power; it is sown a natural body, it is raised a spiritual body.
>
> 1 Corinthians 15:42-4

(c) The resurrection body belongs to a different order from the body in which we now live. It is of the earth, it *will be* heavenly (1 Cor. 15:48). Paul works this distinction out in terms of the two humanities to which the Christian has belonged. He was 'in Adam' and therefore shares in all the characteristics of Adam's existence as man and sinner. So he lives in a natural, earthy body. He has borne his likeness. But by grace he will also bear the likeness of the second Man and Last Adam, the Lord Jesus Christ. His new body will therefore be utterly changed from his present body. It will be in all its characteristics like Christ's resurrection body—fitted to a new kind of existence altogether. It will not be a natural body (fit for this natural world) but a spiritual body (fitted for that realm in which the Spirit reigns in the believer).

That is why Paul unveils the future resurrection day momentarily:

> We will not all sleep, but we will all be changed—in a flash, in the twinkling of an eye, at the last trumpet. For the trumpet will sound, the dead will be raised imperishable, and we will be changed. For the perishable must clothe itself with the imperishable, and the mortal with immortality. When the perishable has been clothed with the imperishable, and the mortal with immortality, then the saying that is written will come true: 'Death has been swallowed up in victory.'
>
> 1 Corinthians 15:51-4

'We will all be changed'! We may only have analogies to help us touch the reality of what will happen to us. But the prospect is thrilling no matter how dimly we see it.

(iii) The regeneration

The language of the New Testament invites us to see a close connection between the inauguration of Christ's reign in the life of the individual and the manifestation of that reign universally in the final transformation of all things. Both are referred to as 'regeneration', or 'renewal' (cf. Matt. 19:28; Tit. 3:5). They too are related to one another as a seed to a flower. Scripture hints that the day of the Christian's glorification will also be the day when the universe in which he lives will be transformed. It is wearing out like a garment and will be rolled away and changed (Ps. 102:26; Heb. 1:11–12). Just as the believer will be changed, so too his environment must be changed to suit his new condition. So the books of 2 Peter and Revelation bear witness to the new heavens and new earth in which righteousness dwells (2 Pet. 3:13; Rev. 21:1 ff). Then 'the creation itself will be liberated from its bondage to decay and brought into the glorious freedom of the children of God' (Rom. 8:21). Paul pictures creation like a woman in travail about to give birth to new life! That new birth will take place at the regeneration. We need to catch the power of this picture, as J. B. Phillips has done so beautifully in his translation of Paul's words:

> The whole creation is on tiptoe to see the wonderful sight of the sons of God coming into their own. The world of creation cannot as yet see reality, not because it chooses to be blind, but because in God's purpose it has been so limited—yet it has been given hope. And the hope is that in the end the whole of created life will be rescued from the tyranny of change and decay, and have its share in that magnificent liberty which can only belong to the children of God.
> Romans 8:19–21

It is this cosmic prospect which is made possible because Christ has drawn the sting of death by his death. He has dealt with the source of man's alienation from God in his sin—and thereby has dealt with the cause of the bondage of all creation. It is his purpose that not only God's children should enjoy liberty from sin's dominion and presence, but that all creation should rejoice in his grace:

You will go out in joy and be led forth in peace; the mountains and hills will burst into song before you, and all the trees of the field will clap their hands. Instead of the thornbush will grow the pine tree, and instead of briers the myrtle will grow. This will be for the Lord's renown, for an everlasting sign, which will not be destroyed.

Isaiah 55: 12–13

(iv) The consummation of our sonship

God's basic and ultimate purpose, as we have now seen in a variety of ways, is that his children should be conformed to Christ in order that he might be the first-born, the elder brother, among many brethren (Rom. 8:29). Christ is the first-born, not only in the sense of his eternal sonship, but also in terms of his resurrection and the glory which he entered through it. In this sense, as the 'firstborn from among the dead' (Col. 1:18), Christ intends to fashion our resurrection life on the model of himself, just as our present life on earth as Christians is shaped by the principles of his ministry too.

We are God's sons now. But creation itself is waiting 'for the sons of God to be revealed' (Rom. 8:19), 'coming into their own' as J. B. Phillips renders it. There is yet more to sonship therefore than regeneration and adoption.

This is, in fact, precisely the point made in the First Letter of John. We are sons, he says, by divine declaration in adoption. More than that, we have been given a new nature in regeneration—it is not merely a legal fiction that we are called God's children. But there is more to come:

> How great is the love the Father has lavished on us, that we should be *called* children of God! And that is what we *are*!
>
> Dear friends, now we are children of God, and what we will be has not yet been made known. But we know that when he appears, we shall be like him, for we shall see him as he is.
>
> 1 John 3:1–2

God will then complete the work he has begun in us, and we will both manifest and enjoy the fulness of fellowship and family life with him. Neither sin nor bodily weakness nor the mind of the flesh will hamper us in expressing the totality of our love for him in worship or the depths of our loyalty to him in obedience and service! It is a glorious prospect. How often children look back on the memory of a father whom they loved but to whom they rarely, if ever, expressed the feelings they had for him, and regret that now no opportunity exists to do so. It is not like that for the child of God. His life has been touched by grace, and he begins to express his love—but oh, so feebly. Yet this is the prospect held out before him: the day is coming when freed from all the hindrances of the flesh, he will be able truly to love and praise his heavenly Father:

> *High is the rank we now possess;*
> *but higher we shall rise;*
> *Though what we shall hereafter be*
> *is hid from mortal eyes.*
>
> *Our souls, we know, when he appears,*
> *shall bear his image bright;*
> *For all his glory, full disclos'd,*
> *shall open to our sight.*

It is this biblical instruction which makes every Christian anticipate the dawning of that coming day, and encourages him to sing with Wesley:

> *Finish then Thy new creation:*
> *Pure and spotless let us be;*
> *Let us see Thy great salvation,*
> *Perfectly restored in Thee.*
> *Changed from glory into glory,*
> *Till in heaven we take our place,*
> *Till we cast our crowns before Thee,*
> *Lost in wonder, love, and praise.*

'Then the end will come,' says Paul (1 Cor. 15:24), or, as we might say from a different perspective as we contemplate what it means to stand in resurrection bodies, changed into the likeness of Christ, sharing in the regeneration of all things which will accompany our full sonship 'our adoption as sons, the redemption of our bodies' (Rom. 8:23)—'Then the beginning will come.' Then shall we enter into the world of eternal light and glory and joy!